TREES
IN YOUR
GROUND

THE TREE COUNCIL

FOREWORD

The urban tree is at a cross-roads. On one side stands development that regards its tangle of roots as a threat to the increasingly dense subterranean infrastructure. On another stands the equally grave threat of escalating carbon emissions and the capacity of the tree to absorb some of them. From a third side comes the urgent need to ameliorate the concrete urban sprawl, or even the rural townscape, by a huge increase in tree planting. The vast majority of us live in urban or suburban circumstance in Britain. I do so myself. I must confess that my own small London plot is almost certainly 'over-treed'. Two acacias that I planted when I moved in twenty six years ago now tower above the roof.

A national drive to plant more trees, encompassing individuals, communities and local authorities, could have a fantastic effect on most neighbourhoods, urban and rural alike. The trouble is that most people have no idea of what they, as individuals, could do to make it happen. I hope that 'Trees in Your Ground' will help provoke that revolution in tree planting - perhaps less haphazardly than my own example. I hope too that it will raise the profile of the tree right up on the planning agenda. Indeed I believe the tree should be at the very heart of 'planning gain'. More, that no new build or major refurbishment of buildings with a street frontage should be permitted without additional tree planting accompanying the plans.

With The Tree Council, I've been exploring another way of ensuring more trees, promoting the principle that where street works are carried out, companies should liaise with the local community to agree the planting of, say, at least one street tree for around twenty metres of dig. It would not be expensive. The average tree, mature enough for street planting, can cost less than £25 when bought commercially from reputable tree suppliers. Where appropriate, the company that is doing the digging may be able to use its plant and maps of the substructure to place and dig the tree pits. The Tree Council's volunteer Tree Wardens could play a facilitative role in their communities, encouraging the involvement of local people whilst co-ordinating the planting and after-care with the local authority.

Mitigation of climate change impact combined with aesthetic urgency compel us to plant more trees in our ground. If a country like Ireland can devise a plan for reducing plastic bag use by 90% and put it into action; if the same country can ban smoking in public places - surely with our resources we in Britain, can transform our urban landscape inside a decade. I hope this publication will help to ensure a huge uplift in the number of trees in our ground.

Jon Snow, October 2005.

Trees in your ground can significantly improve
the appearance of your neighbourhood.

CONTENTS

Below: Magnolias make a beautiful focal point for a garden.

TREES IN YOUR GROUND MATTER

Most people, if they stop to think about it, would agree that trees matter to the quality of the environment, whether in the countryside, suburbs or inner cities. Many neighbourhoods could do with more trees, yet often existing trees are felled for development, damaged at their roots by digging, starved of moisture, vandalised, or just generally neglected.

There is still a long way to go to get everyone to recognise the importance of trees, appreciate their real value and realise that there is much that they themselves can do to cherish the trees growing in 'their ground' and to plant more of them.

That is why The Tree Council is asking people to take a long hard look at how much trees contribute to anywhere they consider to be their patch — places where they live, work, learn or enjoy themselves. As always, The Tree Council is enlisting the support of its member organisations and its volunteer Tree Wardens, not only to develop their own work for trees, but also to spread the Trees in Your Ground message.

The aim of this book is to help everyone to:

- value the trees growing in their neighbourhoods

- plant more trees in their own gardens

- work with others to get more trees planted at work, school, along streets, in neighbouring gardens and in public or private parks

- choose the right tree for the right place

- ensure that all newly planted trees get the aftercare they need to thrive

Until quite recently, the values attached to trees and woods were very straightforward. In the countryside they produced timber and some habitat for wildlife, while in towns they were valued almost entirely for their beauty. Now there is a growing recognition that trees and woods also provide a wide variety of other benefits, which are particularly important to the quality of life for the millions of people who live and work in Britain.

They provide summer shade in a time of increasing climate change and also stabilise the soil. They are good for our health by reducing stress and air pollution. As well as providing fruit, timber and renewable fuel, trees have economic benefits: they help to create jobs, encourage inward investment as employees choose workplaces in attractive surroundings and increase house values. Trees also strengthen communities by providing opportunities for people to work together for the benefit of 'their' trees and the local environment in general.

Everyone can do something to green their patch. Anyone lucky enough to have a garden can take direct action to plant new trees. Elsewhere – in neighbourhood streets, open areas or parks, at workplaces or in school grounds – people can have influence, but usually do not have the right to carry out planting themselves. They may need to act as a local tree advocate, by persuading other people and helping them to understand the importance of planting the 'right trees' in their ground.

"Suburbs are places where developers
bulldoze out all the trees, and then
name the streets after them."
William Vaughn

People want to live and work in healthy,
attractive, comfortable surroundings, and trees
greatly enhance the local environment in our
towns and cities. They should not be regarded as
an optional extra there, but as a necessity.

The UK is one of the world's most urban societies
and there is a pressing need to bring more of the
benefits of trees to where most people live and
work – in towns and cities. Trees in urban design
are an important aspect of Britain's heritage, and
respect for the cultural past should influence
decisions about the future.

By planting trees in your ground, you can play an
active role in improving the environment in your
neighbourhood, making your local patch a better
place to live.

Here are some of the benefits of trees and woods:

- Trees have an impact, if only modest, on global warming

- Trees slow down wind speed substantially

- Trees cut down air pollution from the burning of fossil fuels

- Trees reduce the impact of rainstorms

- Trees reduce summer temperatures in towns and cities

- Trees and woods in towns make a very positive contribution to people's health by reducing stress.

- The canopies of trees act as a filter for particulate pollution

- Trees absorb gases such as carbon monoxide, nitrogen dioxide and sulphur dioxide through their leaves

- Trees can reduce noise levels by as much as 6 to 8 decibels

- Trees can create jobs in planting and aftercare, and for local rangers in helping the local community to gain maximum enjoyment from the trees on their doorstep

- Trees act as traffic calmers when they line urban roads

- Trees provide shade

- A tree-rich urban landscape is increasingly recognised as an important attraction for new businesses

- Studies have also shown that house values are higher where property is associated with mature trees.

Trees in cities help to cut down pollution, making a healthier environment. They also make property sales a more attractive proposition by their presence…

… and are most useful for screening industrial buildings, as well as being invaluable for shade.

A tree-lined suburb of Denver provides valuable shade for local residents and their homes.

To change the value that is placed on Britain's trees, many more people need to understand the benefits that trees bring. Fortunately Britain has a nucleus of caring people passionately prepared to protect trees when they are threatened, but we must encourage this force to grow and become increasingly vocal in praise of trees. Currently their efforts reflect, and are partly modelled on, the outcome of research into the value of trees initiated in America some years ago.

In the late 1980s, after much political pressure from voluntary tree organisations, the US Federal Government decided to sell to the general public the message that 'trees are good'. Scientists working for the US Forest Service drew on data from three aspects of research into the "Value of Trees":

- the monetary value of trees (in Sacramento)

- the 'social aspects' of trees (in Chicago)

- the air quality value of trees (in New York)

Information from this research was presented as a statement of the benefits that accrue as a result of the presence of trees in your neighbourhood and city.

To raise the profile of trees, the Federal Government and other bodies began to use the following promotional ideas:

SHADE

In the generally hot climate of the USA, the air-conditioning unit is ubiquitous, often standard in cars and buildings. Running units costs money and often puts strains on power generators during peak demand. It was calculated that trees strategically placed to shade buildings could reduce a household's electricity demand by up to 30%. In consequence, saving money by planting shade trees has become one of the leading promotional messages about trees in the USA.

PROPERTY VALUES

"A street with trees is nicer than one without". Unfortunately this statement was not seen to have a great practical value. Consequently researchers attempted to put a value on the presence of trees. They calculated that a potential increase of between 5 and 15% to a property if it had trees around it. Thus the American public can appreciate trees as a good investment, because they increase the value of their homes.

REPLACEMENT VALUES

The USA Council of Tree and Landscape Appraisers places a notional replacement value on trees. This is the most widely used protection device for trees on public land, because it enables the city arborist to determine a financial value for any tree. A developer has to pay the city that amount for the right to remove it. This money then goes into planting new trees on city-owned land.

In the USA, replacement value is important because it enables everyone to recognise the financial value of a tree. These replacement values have been used both for individual trees and to place a value upon the trees of whole cities. There are 6 million trees in the 2580 km² (995 square miles) of Sacramento County, California. Using the replacement value system, the trees of Sacramento were valued at $12.6 billion in 1996. Each year as the trees grow their value increases by another $665 million – in banking or business terms that is the interest on the investment.

The Forest Service research branch has also estimated that these trees produce annual savings of:

- $25 million in air conditioning costs
- $36 million in pollutant uptake (1,770 metric tons)
- $3.1 million through uptake of atmospheric carbon dioxide

These figures are all used by tree organisations in the US to promote the concept that trees are not only 'nice', but have an economic and personal importance. This has raised the profile of trees. Because of voter pressure, the politicians are made directly aware of the importance of trees, resulting in valuable budgets being spent to improve tree stocks and engage the public further with trees.

The consequence of these budgets and all the tree-focussed activity in the USA is that at all levels within the US system there are groups working to produce a tree-rich environment, and all are seeking community-wide involvement.

Trees in downtown Seattle provide visual relief amongst the skyscrapers and act as green lungs in the city.

> "The materials of city planning are sky, space, trees, steel and cement, in that order and that hierarchy"
> Le Corbusier

In Britain slower progress has been made in raising the awareness of the value trees have to towns and cities. In 1999 and again in 2005 The National Urban Forestry Unit (NUFU) published "Trees Matter", a review showing that trees have 'value', which can be summarised as follows:

URBAN ENVIRONMENT

- Trees soften the often very austere landscapes of towns and cities, making them greener and more attractive

- Trees can save up to 10% of energy consumption through their moderation of the local climate. They also stabilise the soil, prevent erosion, reduce the effects of air pollution and storm water run-off and are a mainstay in land reclamation.

- The canopy of the urban forest plays a valuable role by intercepting rain which then either drips gradually to the ground, or evaporates back into the atmosphere, so reducing the risk of flash-flooding.

- Establishing trees and woodland on derelict, degraded and contaminated land is inexpensive and can greatly improve its appearance, enhancing its value to wildlife and recreation.

WILDLIFE

- Trees are a vital component of the urban ecosystem. They support a great variety of wildlife which people can enjoy close to home.

- Urban woodland is close to where people live and work, offering opportunities for environmental education and popular pastimes such as bird watching. It also acts as a reservoir for a great deal of the wildlife in private gardens from which people gain so much enjoyment.

HEALTHIER LIVES

Trees reduce the effects of two major scourges of modern society – respiratory disease and stress-related illness.

- Particles from smog and other pollutants irritate sufferers' airways. Tree canopies act as a filter for pollution. The fine particles trapped on the surfaces of leaves could otherwise exacerbate diseases such as asthma and bronchitis.

- Trees reduce smog formation and, by shading out a key ingredient, solar radiation. They therefore have a positive impact on asthma and other allergic conditions.

- Gases such as carbon monoxide, nitrogen dioxide and sulphur dioxide are known to cause respiratory problems. Trees absorb these gases through their leaves, yet again reducing the effect on sufferers from respiratory conditions.

- The stress of life in urban Britain is very significant in the health of the nation and many people find a green environment more relaxing. Urban residents suffering from stress experience less anger, sadness and insecurity when viewing tree-rich surroundings.

- Trees provide an attractive, calm setting for recreation, encouraging healthy exercise and combating stress-related illnesses.

PROPERTY VALUES

■ Several studies, principally in North America, have shown that average house prices are between 5% and 18% higher where property is associated with mature trees.

LOCAL ECONOMY

■ Trees, even in towns, yield traditional products such as timber and fruit, whilst emerging commercial products such as wood chip mulch, renewable fuel and even the chemical extract for an anti-cancer drug have a value and are now helping to finance urban tree and woodland management.

■ Employers are increasingly recognising that the quality of the work-place is important. A tree-rich urban landscape is attractive for new businesses and those relocating and these, in turn, can create employment.

OPEN SPACE MANAGEMENT COST SAVINGS

■ Developing woodland cover as an alternative to grass that is currently close-mown several times a year has been shown to reduce annual maintenance costs while providing recreational open space capable of absorbing many more people at any one time.

COMMUNITY

■ People derive satisfaction from growing and planting trees, caring for them and sharing the experience. This builds a strong sense of ownership, helps reduce vandalism and increases the sense of individual and communal achievement.

■ Easy access to trees and woodland provides a vital facility for both formal and informal learning in the urban environment.

"Trees Matter" is an excellent summary of the current arguments for the value of trees. However these messages need to be reinforced with the public so that British people value the "trees in their ground".

A tip site behind a colliery in South Wales has been planted with conifers. This commercially valuable plantation also helps to soften the landscape.

> "One generation plants the trees under which another takes its ease"
> Chinese proverb

As an umbrella body for organisations working together for trees, The Tree Council has been working for 30 years on projects to engage and educate the public about trees and their value in everyone's patch. Two key ways it does this are through its:

- countrywide Tree Warden Scheme
- annual programme of public involvement initiatives

THE TREE WARDEN SCHEME

Tree Wardens are community-based volunteers who are enthusiastic supporters of trees and are prepared to devote time to champion them. After training, Tree Wardens become involved in gathering information, local liaison, practical projects and protecting trees. These four roles are the core of the scheme and obvious environmental benefits are gained from involving the community in these endeavours.

The Scheme is effectively a large-scale environmental education programme, teaching individuals about the value of trees and using them as agents within their communities to promote trees for the well-being of everybody.

ANNUAL PROGRAMME

To endorse the message that 'trees matter' and to raise awareness of this among as wide an audience as possible, the Tree Council has initiated and annually co-ordinates four major events in the environmental calendar:

- **Seed Gathering Season** (September/October) – encouraging the public to collect seeds and grow their own trees for eventual planting on sites (with the owners' permission)
- **National Tree Week** (end of November/beginning of December) – launching the winter tree planting season and celebrating trees and woods
- **Trees Love Care** (March to September) – focusing on essential aftercare of new trees for five years after planting until they become self-sufficient, and ensuring that they do not suffer from neglect
- **Walk in the Woods** (throughout May) – encouraging people to visit woods when most people consider they are at their most beautiful.

During an average National Tree Week up to half a million people undertake some form of project or tree planting: evidence of keen public interest.

The Tree Warden Scheme and the annual programme provide continuing opportunities to promote trees and woods to the public. However, if the public is to become fully engaged with trees, there needs to be:

- a wider understanding of the value trees have to individuals and their communities
- the development of new community-based conservation initiatives with trees at their heart
- a raising of the political profile of the role of trees and their value

If Britain's residents can see the value of trees in their ground, then the future is healthy. If not then their interest and concern for trees will decline and trees might gradually disappear from our towns, cities and countryside because they would be seen as a 'nuisance' and a financial liability.

If Britain's towns and cities are to have a green and healthy future, the value of trees must be promoted whenever possible and wherever possible – at work, in our streets and in our gardens.

A Tree Warden, using the latest technology in the field, records problems with a suburban tree.

"The tree which moves some to tears of joy is in the eyes of others only a green thing which stands in the way."
William Blake

For many, especially residents of inner cities, housing estates and other densely populated areas, trees planted along streets and in local parks, community gardens, city farms and other communal green areas are often the only ones they encounter in their daily lives. These trees not only enhance an otherwise austere landscape, but also provide a better environment for recreation and valuable habitats for wildlife.

However, trees in private gardens are increasingly important. There are an estimated 25 million homes in the UK Of these, 15 million have gardens covering a total of between 0.4 and 1.2

One of the most frequently chosen species for London's gardens is the Lawson cypress.

million hectares (1-3 million acres). These gardens provide many children with their first experience of wildlife and give others the opportunity to play outdoors. Not surprisingly, gardening is extremely popular and a major media focus. The Royal Horticultural Society has over 300,000 members, the Chelsea Flower Show attracts 157,000 visitors and the BBC Gardeners' World programme has more than 3 million viewers an episode (during 2005).

Despite this interest, little research has been undertaken on the role of trees in Britain's gardens. However, recent research in Sheffield has shown that private gardens account for an amazing 23% of the city's area (about 3300 hectares or 8100 acres). While the average garden is just over half the size of a tennis court, the Sheffield researchers found an estimated 360,000 trees growing in the city's gardens.

Sheffield's enormous acreage of private gardens is critical for wildlife in the city. The research found that the number of trees and large shrubs was the single most important contribution to the abundance of invertebrates. Garden trees can therefore be seen to play a critical role in the biodiversity and ecological value of a city.

In neighbouring Wakefield, garden trees cover 1.3% of the city, some 429 hectares (1060 acres), while in London research in the 1990s showed that 64% of the capital's trees were privately owned – a staggering 3,840,000 trees, mostly growing in gardens.

The total tree stock of London – private and public trees together – comprised 240 different species, although almost 20% of the total population was made up of two species – Lawson cypress (10.4%) and sycamore (6.7%).

The other common trees were ash (3.5%), London plane (2.6%), wild cherry (2.6%), Leyland cypress (2.4%), silver birch (2.4%), hawthorn (2.2%), holly (2.2%), Norway maple (2.1%), lime (2.1%), myrolbalm plum (2.1%) crab apple (1.8%) and English oak (1.8%).

Analysing the data for only the residential trees showed that cherries, cypresses, apples and maples were the most common trees, amounting to over 50% of the total. Unfortunately this predominance of a very small range of species may not be maximising the contribution that could be made by garden trees to the visual amenity and wildlife value of London.

So it can be seen that:

- gardens occupy a large proportion of a city's land area
- gardening is a much enjoyed pastime
- garden trees are abundant, often the largest percentage of a town or city's trees
- garden trees contribute greatly to the biodiversity of a city
- garden trees often come from a restricted range of species

These conclusions suggest that Britain's gardeners could contribute greatly to the landscape and ecological value of our cities through their choice of tree species. However, before planting, careful thought should be given to the characteristics and qualities that a tree can bring and it would appear that currently insufficient care is being taken when choosing Britain's garden trees.

PRE-ROMAN TIMES

The relationships between ancient Britons and their trees during pre-Roman history can only be deduced from archaeological evidence. Our view has been largely shaped by the finds unearthed in Mesolithic and Neolithic sites. There is no doubt that timber was used to build dwellings, fashion weapons and tools, construct stockades or hedges, as well as a source of fuel. Midden contents, which often contain seeds, reveal that the fruits of wild trees were regularly consumed either as food or the constituents of various 'home brews'.

Because little is known about tree planting during this period, the assumption has usually been that tree products were simply gleaned from whatever grew locally. However, around 5,000 years ago there was a move away from the nomadic lifestyle. People began to build permanent settlements and to clear land which they could farm. If these people were no longer travelling to find the trees and plants they needed for themselves and their livestock they had to adopt a regime of planting and tending in order to maintain self-sufficiency.

The assumption must be that tree maintenance was principally functional – i.e. that certain species were encouraged for their specific timber uses, foods and medicines. Large broadleaf trees were also probably retained as shade and fodder for livestock. If the people of pre-Roman Britain planted trees simply for their aesthetic appeal or as part of garden schemes around their homesteads then there is currently no evidence to support this.

ROMAN TIMES

Roman writers and early Irish literature reveal that for many centuries the Celtic peoples had strong spiritual affiliations to trees, reflected in their rune script known as Ogham. The eighteen characters of the Celtic alphabet all represent trees and that is the basis of the modern Irish alphabet. The first three Celtic characters are B (Beth), L (Luis) and N (Nion), which signify birch, rowan and ash. To the Celts all trees had their meaning. To the Druids the oak was the most sacred of trees, revered for its strength and longevity. Both Celt and Roman alike held the oak sacred, so it is hardly surprising that large oaks often became important meeting places or boundary markers. The oak also had many medicinal benefits.

Sweet chestnut, introduced by the Romans, has become one of Britain's most familiar broadleaf trees.

A long tradition of embracing the spirituality of trees has led to their planting and nurturing in close association with settlements, but exactly how far back in history is difficult to ascertain. Both holly and rowan are reputed to ward off evil spirits and black magic, and even to this day may

The reconstructed Roman garden at Fishbourne Palace in Sussex shows the use of box, pergolas for vines, and trellises for fruit trees.

be found growing close to cottages in some rural regions. However the numerous medicinal virtues of most of our native trees must have been a good enough reason to plant them close to the home.

Soon after the Romans arrived in Britain they brought some of their most useful trees and other plants to support their existence in these cold northern climes. They are credited with the introduction of sweet chestnut – valued for its nutritional nuts and useful coppice wood – and walnut, which was eaten and often pressed for its oil. They also introduced stone pine (*Pinus pinea*), presumably for pine nuts with their salads.

The Romans built fine villas and to augment their grand designs they planted formal gardens to remind them of home. There are records of incredible box topiary in the gardens of Rome

and, because box was a readily available native tree in Britain, it is reasonable to suggest that British villas were similarly adorned.

The Romans also brought orchard culture to these shores. They had discovered wonderful sources of fine fruit tree varieties across the Caucasus. They planted groves of apples, pears (Pliny the Elder, writing in the first century, knew of 39 varieties) and plums. The seeds of Britain's great gardening culture had been sown.

Above: Fine spreading yew trees surround a country church in Gloucestershire.

Opposite: Clipped Irish yews adorn the famous churchyard at Painswick. A 19th century discovery in County Fermanagh soon became the ideal compact substitute for the common yew in innumerable churchyards throughout Britain.

SIGNIFICANCE OF THE YEW

For the past two thousand years one particular tree has been growing slowly but steadily in many corners of Britain, and it is the extreme vintage of the ancient yews which gives rise to many conundrums concerning their origins. Were these trees planted in a specific place for a specific reason? Were they simply naturally occurring trees which became adopted as spiritual totems and landmark trees? Were they, as some have supposed, the early markers for saint cells? Many yews grow by old springs or wells, so were they markers for these? There are no definitive answers, but many of our ancient yews could be at least 2,000 years old, and a handful may be even older than this.

A long-standing traditional reverence for the yew stems from its association with immortality, arising from its evergreen fronds and venerable life span. This reverence held great sway with the Celts and other pre-Roman peoples across Europe. When St. Augustine and the early Christian missionaries were despatched to Britain by Pope Gregory the Great they were ordered not to destroy the heathen temples, some of which most certainly were amongst yew groves or close to great old yew trees. Instead, the yews were integrated into the new Christian places of worship and the species became synonymous with churches. Gradually, as new churches were built yews were deemed the appropriate tree to plant nearby.

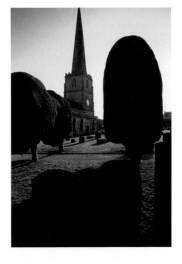

These mighty trees which have endured for centuries in the churchyards of many British villages are clearly the true champion trees in our ground. It has been fortunate that their sacred locations have aided their care and conservation at the focal point of many a settlement.

It is interesting to note that the yew, which has always been more prolific in the southern and western counties of England and in Wales, has left relatively few examples of its presence in today's place names. When the name is evident, in many cases there are no longer any yews in the vicinity.

OTHER PROMINENT SPECIES

In Anglo-Saxon charters of the 10th century there are many fascinating and detailed accounts of perambulations around parcels of land or parishes (beating the bounds) where individual and specifically named trees were a very regular feature, most especially in the hedgerows. Dr. Oliver Rackham discovered that certain trees were recorded more than others. Thorn (hawthorn) was most frequently mentioned, whether due to its abundance and/or longevity. During May (a popular time for beating the bounds) the hawthorn is in flower and would thus stand out in the landscape. As would be expected, oak features prominently too, and also crab apple, willow, elder and alder. Lime, birch and beech, predominantly woodland species, feature much less.

The delightful descriptions of many of these trees – crooked, prostrate, hollow, burry or lichen-covered – underline the intimate knowledge which a community possessed of its surroundings and the importance of these natural forms in the lives and legal processes of each village. It seems strange to note that holly and yew, two evergreen species which would seem to offer perpetual markers in the landscape, are rarely mentioned.

Gospel Oaks were a frequent inclusion in charters. These were large oaks beneath which a minister might preach to his parishioners, particularly during beating the bounds ceremonies. Large oaks became prominent for a variety of reasons – trysting trees for lovers, meeting places for courts, county boundary markers – and hollow oaks might be used to imprison thieves and poachers, whilst Bull Oaks were ideal for penning bulls or other livestock.

Most British place names were established before the Norman Conquest. A glance at any map today instantly shows how important trees were through the preponderance of tree-related names, not only of villages, but also of rivers, landscape features, farms, houses and inns.

This familiarity with native trees was born out of deep understanding of how fundamental they were for survival. Without trees there was no timber for building, no bark to tan leather, no fuel for the fire, no handles for tools and weapons, no fruits and nuts to augment the diet, and none of the medicinal benefits.

Following the Norman Conquest it is clear that trees were being planted throughout the medieval period, but details are sketchy. As Hugh Johnson amusingly asserts, the study of plants (and trees) in the Middle Ages, "lapsed into a mixture of carpenter's know-how, herbalist's mumbo-jumbo and poetical symbolism".

Typical tumbling form of an old black mulberry, an introduction in the early 16th century from the Caucasus.

Prior to 1500 there was little information about tree planting or selection of species, but after the Roman withdrawal very few new trees arrived in Britain. It is thought that the sycamore, an inveterate coloniser, arrived from northern Europe some time after the late 13th century, although no specific date can be identified. Its influence on the British landscape continues to be immense. Equally, the arrival of the horse chestnut from Turkey around 1600 was the beginning of an entertaining relationship with a characterful tree. Here, if ever there was one, is a children's delight. Sticky buds burst into vivid green downy foliage. Great cream candles of flower spikes become shiny brown

conkers to pitch for and battle with. However, this non-native still has its band of detractors.

It was not until 1523, when Fitzherbert published his 'Book of Husbandry', that a written work explained exactly how people might plant and manage trees. Further valuable plant information became accessible in the early English herbals. William Turner published his illustrated 'Herbal' in three parts between 1551 and 1568. At long last a comprehensive work on the recognition of plants and their associated medicinal virtues was available. This was followed in 1597 by John Gerard's 'Herball'.

The following century John Parkinson published his 'Paradisi in sole Paradisus terrestris' in 1629. He was an enthusiastic gardener and plant collector who was keen to pass on his wealth of experience and knowledge. However, it was with the publication of John Evelyn's 'Sylva – A Discourse on Forest Trees' in 1662 that a dedicated work for those who would plant trees became available. Evelyn went into the minutest detail of how to nurture various species successfully and, with the commercial forester in mind, set forth the virtues of the timber and the expectations of their harvest potential. So comprehensive was this work that it went to several editions for over a century.

INTRODUCTION OF NEW SPECIES

Meanwhile the plant hunters had begun to sally forth to distant shores, returning with all manner of natural booty. In the mid 16th century the eastern plane arrived from the Caucasus, and was destined to find fame as the perfect mate for the western plane, one of the earliest arrivals from the Americas in the 1620s. The result – the ubiquitous London plane.

The first hybrid is generally thought to date from 1663 in Britain, and it is highly likely that the cross occurred in the Lambeth garden of the famous 17th century gardener and plant hunter John Tradescant, as it is known that both species were growing there. Thenceforth London plane became one of the most important urban trees in the country. Fast growing, graceful, resistant to pollution and resilient in the face of hard pruning, this tree has it all. It is estimated that around 50 per cent of trees in the streets and squares of Britain's capital are London planes. The oldest, in Berkeley Square, are more than 200 years old.

In 1638 the first Lebanon cedar seed was brought to Britain from Syria by Dr. Edward Pococke,

and tradition has it that he planted one in his rectory garden at Childrey in Oxfordshire in 1646. The magnificent tree still thrives and represents a garden icon for the following two centuries. Stately homes, country mansions, municipal parks and even some lesser properties, which never quite calculated the cedar's growth potential, were spurred to plant this tree of great stature and great spiritual significance – for surely everyone knew that King Solomon built his temple from the cedar's timber.

Throughout the 17th century new trees for Britain continued to cross the Atlantic from eastern and central North America. Arguably one of the most handsome was the tulip tree which was admirably suited to the British climate. Foresters were eager to see if these arrivals had commercial potential in their new homes. The quality of tulip tree timber never quite lived up to its American pedigree, so it has generally been planted as an amenity tree – startling in its golden yellow autumnal glory.

Even as the new species from across the world were arriving, the designers of gardens were still using their relatively small portfolio of existing trees. In the late 17th and early 18th centuries the influence of Dutch garden design during the reign of William and Mary brought a renewed passion for topiary, which had been out of vogue for at least a century. Evelyn, in 1662, had promoted yew for topiary as an alternative to the benchmark species – box. In 1694 Guillaume Beaumont began a grand design for Colonel Grahme, at Levens Hall in Cumbria, to create what remains to this day the finest topiary garden in Britain. That it was not swept away by such great landscapers as William Kent and Capability Brown remains a miracle. Fashion has taken garden design through several cycles of intense formality and naturalistic expansiveness over the centuries.

It had been notoriously difficult to gain access to the Far East and to establish trade relations, but the French made minor inroads in China and the Dutch East India Company was permitted to trade with Japan. There the German doctor and botanist Engelbert Kaempfer was able to discover the ginkgo in the 1690s, a tree imported from China, but with origins around the world dating back some 200 million years. It would be 1754 before the first examples reached Britain, and one of those first trees finally ended up, in 1761, as one of the founding specimens in the great botanic gardens at Kew. The Old Lion ginkgo stands resolute to this day.

By the late 18th century trees were beginning to filter back from voyages to the Far East. Over the ensuing hundred years plant collectors reached every corner of the globe, so that by the late 19th century the number of trees known to the western world more than trebled. This was a period of gathering the tree palette which would eventually be used to great effect by our finest landscape architects, such as William Robinson and Gertrude Jekyll, in their splendid garden commissions.

EXOTIC IMPORTATIONS

The early years of the 19th century saw great collaborations of plant hunters, botanists, nurseries and private collectors. The glorious treasure chest of trees on the west coast of North America still lay untapped, until the remarkable diligence, bravery and fanatical energy of David Douglas brought two of Britain's prime timber trees – the Douglas fir and the Sitka spruce – as well as several other maples, firs and pines.

Archibald Menzies had brought the first monkey puzzles from Chile in 1795, but it was William Lobb who, in 1841, reintroduced the tree and Veitch's nursery of Exeter popularised it. The monkey puzzle, the cedar and the Wellingtonia (introduced by Lobb in 1853) became three of the most sought-after specimen trees for impressive centrepieces of many formal gardens.

In the midst of all these exotic importations the great landscapers, such as Charles Bridgeman, William Kent and Capability Brown, were busily transforming parks and gardens into vast rolling landscapes employing man-made 'natural' hills and vales, meandering rivers and tastefully distributed spreading specimen trees or picturesque clumps. Gone were the avenues. Out went the topiary and fussy formality. Naturally occurring native species were the order of the day and the new trees were virtually ignored for this manufactured country-side. An emerging theory suggests that many of the larger specimen trees of parkland were actually hedgerow trees which were retained for the new schemes, when all signs of hedged farmland were obliterated. The linear alignments of many of these trees today may bear out this theory.

By the mid-19th century a sturdy band of aristocratic private plant collectors was beginning to get fired up by the wealth of amazing trees with which they could adorn their stately homes. The Holfords at Westonbirt began their marvellous pleasure garden and arboretum, as did Robert Holford's neighbour, Earl Ducie of Tortworth. Their friend, Earl Somers at Eastnor, in Herefordshire, also began to assemble a splendid collection. Across the land tree collectors were engaged in serious competition to impress, and the drive between estate gateway and front door established both status and botanical erudition.

THE SUBURBAN GARDENER

With such a vast array of trees now available it soon became evident that a reliable source of information for planters was required. John Claudius Loudon was the man to fill this niche. His 'Arboretum et Fruticetum Britannicum' of 1838 was a superb reference work for botanists and gardeners alike. Loudon went out of his way to champion the widespread planting of all the new and varied species from around the world. In the same year he also published 'The Suburban Gardener and Villa Companion', for the owners of even the most modest Victorian residences were getting their hands on the new species they were seeing on their travels around Britain and the continent, or reading about in newspapers and journals.

By the end of the 18th century, churchyards in urban areas could not accommodate the numbers of dead from the increased urban population. Parliament therefore authorised new commercial cemeteries. The first was established in Liverpool in 1825. The landscape designer Loudon promoted the idea that these new cemeteries and other public parks could become botanical gardens for the education of all classes of society. At Abney Park (1840), the trees and shrubs were labelled and it was considered to be the most comprehensive arboretum in London.

A Capability Brown landscape at Blenheim Palace in Oxfordshire incorporates clumps of trees and an impressive lake with the dramatic centre-piece of Vanbrugh's bridge.

If the tree planters and gardeners were galvanised in the 19th century, then today there ought to be a superb legacy of trees which we have inherited. This is partially the case, but the trees in our ground have experienced numerous fluctuations of fortune through the 20th century.

At the grander end of the spectrum a harsh reality has been the ever-spiralling costs of maintaining large houses with their extensive estates. Sadly, hundreds of old properties which were no longer viable either crumbled or were demolished. With their demise went some superb gardens and trees. Fortunately, the best of the bunch, Westonbirt in Gloucestershire, has now become the National Arboretum in the care of the Forestry Commission. A return to the exacting detail of the formal gardens of more than a century before brought avenues, geometric parterres, borders and topiary back into fashion once again, but this time they were not just the preserve of the gentry. Country

cottage and town terrace alike forged their own versions of the grand designs. Owners of tree nurseries across the land rubbed their hands with glee.

PLANTING PUBLIC PARKS AND STREET TREES

The Victorians made important moves in town and city to provide green spaces in rapidly expanding conurbations. Public parks were planted and streets were lined with trees. The aspect became ever more verdant, and just as well, since urban dwellers had to cope with increasing levels of pollution. Unfortunately, by the second half of the 19th century, the effects of air pollution were beginning to have an increasingly deleterious effect on the new tree planting.

Reacting to the effects of increasing urbanisation, Ebenezer Howard formulated the concept of the

Garden City in 1902. Howard's idea was to integrate the built and natural environments more closely. The first new town, Letchworth (1904), was inspired by this concept and was planned around the preservation of existing woods, trees and hedges, along with extensive tree planting. Initially an attempt was made to plant a distinctive species for each new road. For example, almond and red horse chestnut were planted for different streets. The town square was planted with hornbeam, deodar cedar, common beech, Lombardy poplar and Cornish elm.

GARDEN CITIES AND NEW TOWNS

As the concept of the Garden City gradually evolved, new styles of planting emerged in the suburbs, such as planting grass verges with small trees. This was possible because a number of smaller varieties had become available including Japanese cherries and purple plums. Government housing design manuals of the inter-war period (e.g. the 'Tudor Walters Report' of 1919), suggested that trees should be placed, "in positions suitable to the size of their ultimate growth".

The authors were concerned to avoid the constant need for pruning of forest-sized trees planted in confined spaces. However, to have created the space necessary for such large trees would have meant reducing house densities to lower levels than were recommended at the time. The smaller cherry trees thus provided the planners with a species which seemed to suit the new requirements of these towns and were widely used.

Young trees abound in central Milton Keynes.

Dramatic modern architecture surrounded by tree-lined thoroughfares, in Milton Keynes.

PLANNING LAWS

The Town and Country Planning Act forms the legislative basis for the protection of trees in urban areas today. Whilst the first Town Planning Act had been passed in 1909, it was not until the National Parks and Access to the Countryside Act 1949 that local authorities could make planning permissions conditional on trees being planted, and that local authorities themselves were empowered to plant trees on any land in their area. With the increasing vulnerability of trees to urban development, wider powers to protect trees were granted to local authorities by subsequent acts. It is now the duty of local authorities to ensure that conditions are imposed on planning consents for the protection of trees on development sites.

The Garden City concept continued to shape the development of new towns during the 1960s and 1970s. Most new towns have taken advantage of existing woodlands and often large areas of new trees are planted particularly on poorer grade land, to provide amenity and landscape restoration. The towns of Redditch and Warrington were the first to include advance structure planting of tree belts into which the new buildings were to fit.

The 1980s and 1990s saw a number of developments which have focused attention on the numerous benefits which trees provide in towns. The development of new towns has provided the opportunity to design and plan large areas of tree-planting within the urban fabric, to the extent that Milton Keynes and Telford have called themselves "Forest Towns".

GREEN LUNGS OF THE CITY

The existence of large tracts of derelict land in declining industrial areas has provided the opportunity for large-scale planting projects in cities such as Birmingham, Belfast, St Helens and Edinburgh. Associated with this trend has been the growth in interest in the concept of urban forestry, which regards all the trees in an urban area as comprising a 'forest' and manages them for the many benefits they can give, from visual amenity to timber.

To this day most of the community spaces provided by our forebears have remained sacrosanct, which has been an environmental lifeline, since pollution, which might have been expected to decline after the Clean Air Act of the 1960s, has accelerated with the increase in urban road traffic. Trees are most definitely the green lungs of the city, and some can survive the rigours better than others. London plane and common lime have been hardy perennials, but numerous ornamental cherries, crabs and maples have also found their place. (Further alternatives can be found on pages 40 – 69). The pressure on urban trees remains in the face of development, road widening, trenching for utilities and legal concerns over subsidence and health and safety issues.

In rural Britain tree planting had long been part of the country calendar, until the Second World War. Hedge trees were planted or encouraged in order to provide timber, fuel wood, protection and shade. Orchard culture was brisk, with a good demand for fruit (there were few imports), cider and perry manufacture, and even the need for vegetable dyes, provided by such fruits as the damson.

However, after the war there was a progressive move towards intensive agriculture, which saw field systems drastically enlarged at the expense of

An old quarry bordering an industrial estate has been planted with trees and managed for wildlife, thus creating an enjoyable amenity for surrounding city dwellers.

many hedges and their large trees. Orchards began to be less profitable, and government subsidies meant the land could be used for better returns. The demise of traditional orchards continues to this day. The gene pool slowly shrinks, and only orchard enthusiasts and organisations such as the National Apple Collection at Brogdale in Kent can hope to reverse the trend.

Elsewhere matters seem a lot brighter. The work of many Tree Council members and others has engendered an ever-increasing interest and under-standing of trees and their care. The boundless energy and enthusiasm of the Tree Council's volunteer Tree Wardens has also increased tree awareness and a sense of custodianship and pride of trees in local communities across Britain.

TREES IN THE CURRENT AGENDA

The need to protect our surroundings was recognised as long ago as the 1970s, when campaigning voluntary sector organisations raised the importance of the environment, including the nation's treeescapes.

Today many of these organisations advise national government, while local authorities work in partnership with the voluntary sector through local strategic partnerships. In consequence, at the beginning of the 21st century, there is a better understanding of the need to protect and plant trees. Indeed, some areas, including Greater Manchester, have substantially increased their tree cover over the last 20 years, thanks to initiatives like the Red Rose Forest project, one of the 12 Community Forests.

National government has also recognised that the quality of our environment has a substantial impact on our well-being, on the sustainability of our communities and on our prosperity. Maintaining our treescapes is clearly an important part of this, so the government has produced a national forestry strategy, whilst local regions are producing regional strategies to protect trees and plan for future tree planting and maintenance.

Many local authorities have also developed tree strategies and local Biodiversity Action Plans (BAPs) to protect their treescapes. BAPs are a move to record the natural environment and then plan its conservation, and trees feature in some of the priority habitats.

The Office of the Deputy Prime Minister (ODPM) is responsible for the government's plans to build

1.1 million new homes over the next 25 years. It has clearly stated that accessible green space and green corridors will be important to the sustainability of new communities. In deprived urban areas regeneration initiatives including 'Liveability' and the 'Cleaner, Safer, Greener' programme have been developed to provide funding that will improve urban environments. The Tree Council's new initiative to increase Tree Wardening in Britain's more urban areas is also part of the ODPM's push to improve the environment in our cities.

Potential future climate change may well see exotic and unusual pines more frequently chosen for urban situations.

Adjoining streets in a city suburb (photographed from the same viewpoint) showing the contrast between a street totally devoid of trees and one where the view is softened by the inclusion of trees and shrubs.

If one reads all the press coverage about impending climate change the outlook might appear gloomy. It is now inevitable that there will be climate change, as the chemicals that the world has pumped into the ozone layer will bring about global warming, even if we were to drastically reduce greenhouse gas emissions tomorrow. The big questions are: Exactly when will temperatures rise? By how much have they risen already and what effect will there be on our vegetation? The short answer is that we simply cannot be sure.

Some estimates see tangible changes within 10 to 15 years, and a long-term outlook in which the British climate in 50 years' time might resemble that of Bordeaux today. However temperature increases themselves are not the main concern, but rather the extreme climatic conditions which plants will have to endure on a more regular basis in coming years. When extreme drought hit Britain in 1976, trees, other plants (and people) suffered, but the suggestion then was that this was a rare occurrence which might only happen once every two or three hundred years. A generation later we face the possibility of such years arising in close succession. And it is not only drought, as recent years have seen increases in occurrences of violent storms, and it is quite likely that storm damage will take its toll on more and more trees.

The first instinct is to see how our native trees will fare. Beech and birch both suffer in droughts, as does the naturalised sycamore. Beech, being shallow-rooted and often growing on light soils, will probably become stressed in the southern counties. Sycamore, an important tree of northern Britain, might also struggle in the south; there will be those who greet that prospect warmly. If the cover of some of our native species shifts to more northern climes it will be interesting to see what

happens in the spaces they vacate. A mixture of natural succession and intervention planting may well create whole new treescapes.

PLANNING AHEAD

Now is not the time to mourn our projected losses, for they are beyond our control. Instead, we should make some provision for judicious planting selections across southern Britain, given the impending changes. This will mean some difficult choices for ardent advocates of the native species, as it is quite likely that some introduced trees will be the most prudent choices (see pages 40 – 69).

There are numerous other concerns for future trees, which affect commercial foresters and the conservators of ancient woodland, drawing together potential problems from issues such as plant competition and an increased range of insect pests and pathogens. We are already aware of the predations of longhorn beetles and numerous phytoptheras which may be poised to tip some of our tree species into similar declines reminiscent of Dutch elm disease.

However there will be positive aspects to the changes, and one, concerning our native small-leaved lime, has already been observed. Hotter summers are causing the species to set viable seed more often, which might mean limes will extend their range after several hundred years of relative stasis.

Over the past 500 years trees from all over the globe have been brought into Britain where, on balance, the majority of them have thrived, giving us a wealth of commercial timber trees and a startling collection of beautiful amenity trees. For people planting trees in their patch today it is far more important to view the future with constructive optimism, rather than despair.

There is little excuse not to plant trees now, and to do it correctly and with foresight. With a choice of more than 2,500 species which grow happily in most parts of Britain the opportunities for adventurous tree planting in 'your ground' have never been better.

An Indian bean tree could be an ideal choice to cope with future changes in Britain's climate.

THE RIGHT TREE IN THE RIGHT PLACE

When choosing a tree for 'your ground' it is essential to think about the roles the tree will serve. Many objectives can be met at once – good autumn colour, a pleasing shape, shade and wildlife benefits are all possible from a single well chosen tree. The ideal is to plant a tree that can grow to full maturity with little or no tree surgery. Mistakes in planting a tree are long-lasting, expensive and difficult to rectify.

Successfully choosing a tree depends upon about 30 good decisions, half in relation to the tree and half to the site. The overriding consideration is that unborn generations should thank you for it. It is easy to cut down a 'wrong' tree, but it is very difficult to establish a different one in its place if it was part of a planting scheme. Vision and faith are needed from the very start because a sapling that can be held between two fingers could eventually become huge and live for hundreds of years.

Unlike a sundial or a house, which stay the same size, a tree will become progressively larger until maturity. Although this may seem a long time – 80 years for an average oak – a tree will expand at about the same rate as herbaceous garden plants. That is anything from 10cm (4 inches) to one metre (3 feet) per year, depending on species and situation. The difference is that each year a tree stacks up its new growth and becomes even larger. So a 100-year-old tree may be likened to 100 flower beds one on top of the other. Once the tree reaches maturity, its width may continue to increase but its height remains about the same.

Trees set a scene. They are dominant and control the sense of scale, sometimes the sense of seclusion and privacy. According to Humphry Repton, the famous landscape designer, "against the sky, jagged tops of conifers produce a sense of drama, while the cloud-like outlines of bushy-topped trees give an air of serenity".

Trees link land and sky. Without them there is a sense of bleakness. Almost as bleak is the sight of an unfortunate lone tree straining to stay upright against the wind in a vast open space. Better by far to plant a clump of trees, even as few as three or five planted two metres (6 feet) apart, to give mutual support to each other and create a much quicker impact. In addition, the chances of mechanical damage or failure are reduced. One risk is that clumps of trees will not be thinned at

the appropriate time, but it is amazing how well most species adapt to such a cosy, neglected relationship. Bundle plantings (two, three or five trees in the same hole) have been known to thrive for more than 200 years.

A tree chosen for a particular place should be ecologically suited to the site. Sometimes it is best to choose locally grown stock. Some birches, for example, do not take kindly to being moved far north or south of their place of origin. They fail to adapt to a change in day length and do not thrive.

A well chosen tree will grow in tune with nature, even in a city, and contribute to a location's biological balance. Some species are particularly good for birds (hawthorn, holly and bird cherry) and others are important for bees (cherry, small-leaved lime and sweet chestnut). Species that are able to provide shelter of any sort for wildlife contribute greatly to the ecosystem. This may be as simple as breaking the force of the wind or reducing the severity of radiation frost or as complicated as providing a niche for a rare invertebrate or home and food for a moth.

There are many considerations when choosing a tree. This book helps you to make the right decisions.

THE SIZE OF YOUR PATCH

The kind of trees that a garden, urban open space or amenity planting can accommodate depends upon the space available. This does not just mean the proximity of walls, roads or boundaries, but the whole impact the trees may have on the landscape and the people who live in it.

In order to measure how near a tree can be planted to a building or other structure, its potential ultimate height and spread on the site should be calculated. It should not be positioned closer to a building than 80% of its height. Then, if it blows down damage will be minimal.

In a few gardens space is not limiting, but often people have just a small plot. For some tree enthusiasts lack of space may be frustrating and small trees will have to suffice.

An uninterrupted view of neighbouring properties may disappoint, especially if there are drab walls, commercial property or leylandii hedges. However pretty the flower garden may be, it will be subordinate to a feature, perhaps a hideous eyesore, beyond your own control. Having developed a garden at ground level, the only way to improve it further is to go upwards, either with pergolas and climbing plants on trellises or by planting trees.

A substantial garden with plenty of space is required for a large tree such as this Cedar of Lebanon.

When planning the new vertical dimension to a garden, consider:

- will new trees block views or shade out windows as they grow?

- will hard landscape features such as statues, foundations, walls and paths be damaged by expanding roots?

- may branches interfere with overhead wires?

Some large shrubs, such as Daphne, Camellia, Pieris or witch hazel can be trained to good effect to resemble small trees where space is very restricted. However, with care, even a large tree can be accommodated if it is sited correctly and has the right shape and form.

A sense of scale must be applied when planting trees into any landscape. The average human eye has a 27° limit on vertical vision, so a tree 8 metres (26 feet) tall runs out of view unless you are 15 metres (50 feet) from it. A tree that will reach 25 metres (82 feet) tall requires 47 metres (154 feet) of space to be seen it in its entirety. However, not every tree needs to be seen in its entirety, unless it is intended as an eye-catching feature.

Vistas, glades and views between the trees are just as important visually as a well-treed area.

SMALL TREES

Wayfaring tree (*Viburnum lantana*)
Spindle tree (*Euonymus europaeus*)
Redbud (*Cercis canadensis*)
Syrian juniper (*Juniperus drupacea*)
Cockscomb beech
(*Fagus sylvatica* 'Cristata')

MEDIUM TREES

Turkish hazel (*Corylus colurna*)
Field maple (*Acer campestre*)
Manna ash (*Fraxinus ornus*)
Maidenhair tree (*Ginkgo biloba*)
Cucumber tree (*Magnolia acuminata*)
Bay willow (*Salix pentandra*)

LARGE TREES

Common oak (*Quercus robur*)
Black walnut (*Juglans nigra*)
London plane (*Platanus* × *hispanica*)
Tulip tree (*Liriodendron tulipifera*)
Beech (*Fagus sylvatica*)
Ash (*Fraxinus excelsior*)
Cedar (*Cedrus species*)
Algerian oak (*Quercus canariensis*)
Sweet chestnut (*Castanea sativa*)

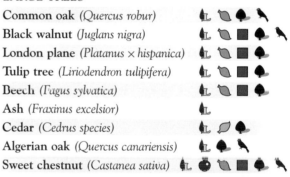

KEY FOR SYMBOLS DEPICTING THE SPECIFIC MERITS OF INDIVIDUAL TREE SPECIES

S	up to 6m	healthy, isolated, specimen in good soil conditions, at 20 years
M	6m to 12m	
L	over 12m	

Flowers

Attractive fruit

Attractive foliage

Attractive foliage (Autumn)

Interesting bark

Shade providing trees

Benefiting wildlife

The eventual height of trees in your garden should always be considered. The birch tree in this garden has quickly grown out of the view from the house and potentially may also cause problems with the overhead wires.

As a tree matures and becomes established it may obstruct a view. If the old view was unpleasant the tree is doing its job but if the view is desirable, either no tree should be planted or it should be managed so it fits into or frames the view. For example, if lower branches are gradually removed the view is revealed again. The appearance of distant sunlit trees, lawns, fields or buildings is enhanced through a shady frame. Blue sky appears more intense when seen behind or fringed by green foliage.

Although a relatively small tree, this rowan softens the lines of the surrounding tower blocks.

THE CITY SCENE

Where massive buildings are clustered in city developments, there is no way that a tree only one tenth of the height of tower block can hide it completely. However, from a human perspective, if you stand under a good sized tree the chances are that you will not see much of the skyscraper on the other side of the street.

Trees provide the eye with a welcome change of shape from the geometric lines of buildings. Nothing yet built has the billowing rounded outline of a tree. In winter the complex random tracery of twigs and limbs serves the same purpose. Winter or summer, glimpses of buildings between trees provide a relief from seeing just the buildings on their own. Clumps of trees in urban open spaces, even churchyards, bring the same visual relief and in addition provide a foothold for wildlife. Birds, in particular, find a place to feed, roost and nest. A town square may be a habitat in which generations of house sparrows spend their entire lives.

CHANGING THE CLIMATE

Trees provide shelter from climatic extremes, especially strong winds. Every tree, however small, creates a microclimate around itself. The slightest easing of the wind, drop of transpired moisture or fleck of shade will be beneficial to something living in the immediate vicinity, not least the tree itself. Trees shield the ground from freezing in winter by insulating a low-level band of air from the open sky above. This is often sufficient to keep night-time soil temperatures just high enough to prevent damaging radiation frost.

Trees purify and moisten the air while absorbing carbon dioxide and city dust. A by-product of their metabolism is life-giving oxygen. For people, one of the most welcome benefits of a tree is summer shade. In America a whole category of species is classified as 'Shade Trees'. Evergreens feature prominently, Osmanthus, Photinia, holly, yew and several conifers being the favourites. Deciduous trees, especially those with broad leaves such as plane, Norway maple, chestnut and whitebeam are some of the best for summer shade. Shade trees should be species that do not harbour sap-sucking aphids or biting insects. Nobody wants to sit in the shade only to be deluged with honeydew and debris or be eaten alive.

Right: A splendid pear tree now stands between an old industrial building and a car park, having become a city feature in the centre of Worcester.

Below: London planes line Pall Mall in London, creating a green space and a wildlife corridor in the heart of the city.

MANAGING SHADE

Trees produce shade. In many circumstances, especially with a changing climate, shade may become an increasingly desirable factor, especially for houses or conservatories where it may be necessary to reduce the heat of hot summers. However, shading flower beds completely for much of the day will often be undesirable. To observe the apparent path of the sun around a garden or planting site and calculate the shadow from a new tree, place a cane or post of known height in the proposed planting position. Measure the length and note the direction of the shadow at various times. Divide the ultimate height of the tree by the height of the cane or post, then multiply the length of the shadow by that number. By carefully locating new trees, shade can therefore be managed to ensure that it occurs where it is desired, and avoided where it is not.

MANAGING WIND

It is better to control wind along the boundary of a planting site with trees than with solid walls or hedges that force the air to rise over the barrier and then continue in a turbulent state. Turbulent air is probably more damaging than the uninterrupted wind would have been – it can tear up plants and rip off roof slates. Trees, particularly deciduous trees in winter when winds are most severe, allow some of the wind to percolate through the branches, dissipating energy as it does so.

Three to five rows of wind-firm broadleaved trees make an ideal windbreak if space is available. They tend to develop a profile with the shortest on the outside, even if the planting is all of one species. This lifts some of the wind up and over the top of the much quieter airflow through the shelterbelt. Turbulence is reduced and concentrated above the level of the protected trees, gardens and buildings.

Protecting trees from wind damage within a planting site depends on choice of species, choice of plant size and aftercare. The best way to keep trees upright is to plant a clump rather than just planting singly. Small plants (e.g. whips) are essential, since it is almost impossible to keep a newly planted standard tree upright if it is exposed. Planting a specimen tree in a clump of shrubs (e.g. tamarisk near the sea) can be successful but care is needed to prevent the shrubs suppressing the young tree or whipping the top out of it.

Sycamores in North Yorkshire are commonly found as protective trees around old farmsteads.

Horse chestnuts are popularly planted as shade and decorative trees in many municipal parks.

TREES FOR COLOUR

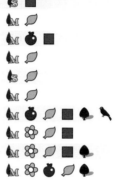

Lace-bark pine *(Pinus bungeana)*

Golden honey locust *(Gleditsia triancanthos* 'Sunburst')

Madrona *(Arbutus menziesii)*

Golden Lawson cypress *(Chamaecyparis lawsoniana* cultivars)

Koster's blue spruce *(Picea pungens* 'Koster')

Robinia pseudoacacia 'Frisia'

Copper beech *(Fagus sylvatica* cultivars)

Smooth Arizona cypress *(Cupressus glabra)*

Oliver's lime *(Tilia oliveri)*

Acer platanoides 'Goldsworth Purple'

WIND FIRM TREES

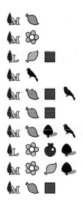

Pin oak *(Quercus palustris)*

Black locust *(Robinia pseudoacacia)*

Eucalyptus (Hardy *species*)

Common alder *(Alnus glutinosa)*

Aspen *(Populus tremula)*

Downy birch *(Betula pubescens)*

Hornbeam *(Carpinus betulus)*

Sycamore *(Acer pseudoplatanus)*

Magnolia (Tree *species*)

Dawn redwood *(Metasequoia glyptostroboides)*

SHADE TREES

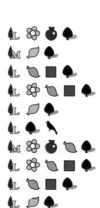

Horse chestnut *(Aesculus hippocastanum)*

Holm oak *(Quercus ilex)*

Beech *(Fagus sylvatica)*

Norway maple *(Acer platanoides)*

Cedar *(Cedrus species)*

Algerian oak *(Quercus canariensis)*

Indian bean tree *(Catalpa bignonioides)*

Tulip tree *(Liriodendron tulipifera)*

London plane *(Platanus × hispanica)*

Lucombe oak *(Quercus × hispanica* 'Lucombeana')

Before choosing it is important to know what features the tree possesses and what features a particular situation requires. Some tree characteristics can be instantly seen (e.g. size, shape, colour and whether evergreen or deciduous). Other features are much more obscure. It may or may not be environmentally valuable. It may smell good or bad; it may even be poisonous.

Timescale may matter, too, since some trees last for hundreds of years while others are short-lived. Find a well established example of the same type growing nearby and observe it closely for as long a period as possible; its good and bad points become obvious in time.

The slow growing tupelo offers superb displays of autumn colour.

Observation is also the best way to research locations. There is no better way to choose a tree for a site than to see what is planted in the surrounding area. Check the existing range of species and how well each is thriving. See if there are trees that are just right for the place – that is, their size is right, the environment is enhanced or the foliage colour and texture complement the surroundings.

Size at maturity is perhaps the most important, and most overlooked feature to consider for a tree in urban surroundings. The most frequent problem occurs when trees become too large for their situation and impinge on surrounding property. By the time this becomes obvious, felling or lopping costs will have soared. Appreciating potential size at the time of planting can be extraordinarily difficult: the sapling is small and it will probably not become excessively large during the planter's lifetime.

Speed of growth is another consideration. The general perception is that trees take generations to become respectably large, but this is not always true. A surprising number of people, and indeed local authorities, are caught out by trees that reach roof height or blot out street lights in just a few years.

Some trees grow fast and never seem to stop (e.g. most poplars). Others grow fairly quickly, but never become excessively large (e.g. black mulberry, field maple, snowy mespil and Swedish whitebeam). These are amongst the most valuable species for garden and urban use, since they soon become established, but never get out of hand.

Commemorative trees can create one of the most difficult circumstances when the donors have provided the actual tree or planting site. The chances of a favourite tree thriving in a predetermined place are usually limited. Many commemorative trees mark either a death or, more happily, a birth. Ideally, a short list of suitable species should be drawn up for a particular site and presented to the donor.

Species may be required for a defined place or purpose, such as a steep slope, or for erosion control, seaside planting, an exposed area or a site that is liable to flooding. Advice is available from professional bodies such as the Environment Agency. In some situations (e.g. floodplains) tree planting may not be permitted. Advice will certainly be required for street planting and for areas where there are likely to be underground services.

FAST GROWING TREES

Silver maple *(Acer saccharinum)*

Tree of Heaven *(Ailanthus altissima)*

Monterey pine *(Pinus radiata)*

Eucalyptus *(Hardy species)*

White willow *(Salix alba)*

Empress tree *(Paulownia tomentosa)*

Caucasian wing nut *(Pterocarya fraxinifolia)*

Wellingtonia *(Sequoiadendron giganteum)*

Modern Hybrid poplars *(Populus × generosa)*

Turkey oak *(Quercus cerris)*

SLOW GROWING TREES

Dogwood *(Cornus sanguinea)*

Box *(Buxus sempervirens)*

Antarctic beech *(Nothofagus antarctica)*

Tupelo *(Nyssa sylvatica)*

Phillyrea latifolia

Tibetan cherry *(Prunus serrula)*

Turner's oak *(Quercus turneri)*

Robinia pseudoplatanus 'Intermis'

Bamboo-leaved oak *(Quercus myrsinifolia)*

Oriental thorn *(Crataegus laciniata)*

SALT TOLERANT TREES

Eucalyptus *(Hardy species)*

Sea buckthorn *(Hippophae rhamnoides)*

White poplar *(Populus alba)*

Blackthorn *(Prunus spinosa)*

Aspen *(Populus tremula)*

Common and Sessile oak *(Quercus species)*

Sycamore *(Acer pseudoplatanus)*

Monterey cypress *(Cupressus macrocarpa)*

Maritime pine *(Pinus pinaster)*

Bishop pine *(Pinus muricata)*

Wellingtonias grow remarkably quickly and must be sited with caution as they will become huge trees.

White poplar is one of the trees to choose where tolerance to salt-laden air is a consideration.

SIZE

In urban landscaping a large tree is traditionally reckoned to be one that normally grows taller than 15 metres (50 feet). A small tree is one that will not grow that high. However, modern gardens tend to be smaller than in earlier times and many will certainly not accommodate a 'small' tree approaching 15 metres (50 feet) high, so a 'very small' category is required. This may well include large woody shrubs probably not exceeding six metres (20 feet) in height.

COLOUR

As a rule bright colours, other than green, are often reserved for urban or amenity sites, while greens are often thought to fit more comfortably into the countryside. Green foliage may be any shade from very dark green (holly and several conifers) to yellow-green (golden Lawson cypress) and grey-green (Koster's blue spruce).

Yellow foliage that lasts all summer is rare; *Robinia pseudoacacia* 'Frisia' is a good example. Red and purple foliage is found on many species including beech, maple and cherry. Variegated foliage occurs in various colours but many of the trees have a sickly appearance and some tend to revert. Quite often, leaf colour will be accentuated by reflection, surface pattern, texture or strongly contrasting leaf undersides. A deep green holly will glitter in sunlight because of its shiny leaves. In a breeze a silver maple will alternate between silver and green as the long-stalked leaves show their backs. Trees with woolly or deeply cut leaves can give a misty impression when viewed from a distance.

Colour choice should depend on whether a seasonal mix is required or the all-year-round constancy of an evergreen would be better. Deciduous trees display very different colours in winter and summer. In winter, beech and hornbeam will often hang on to bright orange-brown rustling dead leaves which are quite unlike their brilliant summer green. Japanese larch is sea-green in summer, straw yellow in the autumn and has a haze of reddish twigs in winter. Bark colour is another feature to consider. Groups of white-stemmed birches, for example, are superb eye-catchers.

SHAPE

Tree profiles vary considerably and respond to environmental forces erratically. Only a few species are totally reliable. Italian cypress, for example, is always rigidly columnar. However a few broad categories are generally accepted (see the list). However each shape can be represented by a deciduous or evergreen example, and this will give a totally different effect.

Pruning trees to produce a particular shape is not recommended. Most will not conform in the same way as a shrub or hedge. Once out of reach of the pruning saw, branches sometimes shoot off in unexpected directions to hideously deform a specimen.

FLOWERS AND FRUIT

Flowering garden trees are a joy if the flowers are low enough to see. However, flowering seasons tend to be short and in some cases the foliage afterwards is disappointing. Fallen petals and debris may also be a nuisance.

Ornamental fruit trees, particularly those not instantly stripped by birds, can provide a brilliant autumn and winter feature. Some flowers and fruit, and indeed some types of foliage, are fragrant or aromatic. It is important to check in advance whether they are likely to induce an allergic reaction.

TREES FOR AUTUMN COLOUR

Tupelo (*Nyssa sylvatica*)

Sweet gum (*Liquidambar stryaciflua*)

Pin oak (*Quercus palustris*)

Hybrid larch (*Larix × marschlinsii*)

Bitternut (*Carya cordiformis*)

Japanese maple (*Acer japonicum & palmatum cvs.*)

Persian ironwood (*Parrotia persica*)

Japanese rowan (*Sorbus commixta*)

Katsura tree (*Cercidiphyllum japonicum*)

Black walnut (*Juglans nigra*)

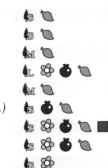

TREE SHAPES (examples)

Columnar (Italian cypress)

Spreading (Horse chestnut)

Rounded (Monterey pine)

Fastigiate (Dawyck beech)

Slender (Serbian spruce)

Weeping (Weeping beech)

Towering (Silver lime)

Massive (Ancient sweet chestnut)

Multi-stemmed (Caucasian wingnut)

Shrubby (Prostrate juniper)

TREES FOR DECORATIVE FRUIT

Wayfaring tree (*Viburnum lantana*)

Rowan (*Sorbus aucuparia and cultivars*)

Holly (*Ilex aquifolium*)

Buckthorn (*Rhamnus cathartica*)

Damson (*Prunus domestica subsp. institia*)

Chinese crab apple (*Malus hupehensis*)

Juniper *cultivars*

Osage orange (*Maclura pomifera*)

Monkey puzzle (*Araucaria araucana*)

Tree of Heaven (*Ailanthus altissima*)

From top: Japanese rowan is an excellent choice for autumn colour; weeping beech has an imposing form; holly and damson produce beautiful fruits in autumn.

LANDSCAPE TREES

Landscape trees enhance the view but not necessarily because of their own particular attributes. In the crudest sense they are dark green blobs on a pale green grassy world. They are usually planted in clumps or roundels to increase impact, particularly when viewed from a distance.

On a smaller scale, in a park or large garden, landscape trees act as a frame or direct the eye towards or away from a feature. Here, at close quarters, species, shape and colour are more relevant. Shape and size can be used to manipulate perspective to some extent: light colours recede into the background and bold-coloured foliage emphasises the foreground. An eye-catching feature or device at the end of a view, often a column or statue, may draw the eye and the feet. However, using a tree for this purpose can be risky because it may change shape during its lifetime or be damaged by wind or lightning.

AVENUES

Few species are suitable for avenue planting. There are excellent examples, but also some glaring examples of what not to plant. A mixture of trees for an avenue can be disastrous. The main difficulty in planning a new avenue is allowing enough space for the ultimate size of the trees. Planting at half spacing with the intention of taking out every other tree seldom works. Removals are seldom done in time or the restriction imposed by having to remove every other tree inevitably means that, to maintain regular spacing, somewhere along the line a misshapen specimen stays and a good one has to go.

SCREENING AND HEDGES

Some trees are ideal as windbreaks and screens from gales, salt-laden air, dust, air pollution and noise (e.g. sycamore, holm oak and Corsican pine). Visual screening can obscure unsightly structures, arterial roads or landfill sites. Tall trees used as hedges are mostly found around hop fields or where soft fruit is grown. It is said that the beneficial effect of this kind of permeable barrier extends downwind a distance of 10 times its height.

INDUSTRIAL SITES

There is an elite group of tough pioneer trees (e.g. alder) that can withstand extreme conditions above and below ground. They are often planted into re-formed reclaimed land or exposed to draughts and turbulence between buildings. On landfill sites they might also be subjected to toxins in the ground and poisonous air. Furthermore, such derelict sites attract high rates of vandalism, fly tipping and theft, so there are advantages in planting a tree that will continue to grow even when it has been smashed and one that does not appear to be worth stealing.

ENVIRONMENTAL CONSIDERATIONS

Planting trees that will complement existing species on or near a site will provide additional habitat for the wildlife already *in situ*. New English oaks (preferably of local origin) near existing trees of the same type, for example, will provide continuity for the many organisms that live on the species. Oaks of dubious provenance may support the wildlife but future generations of oak will be genetically polluted. Introducing alien or especially vigorous trees that compete with existing species of tree or ground vegetation is likely to be environmentally damaging.

TREES FOR AVENUES

Pin oak (*Quercus palustris*)
Hornbeam (*Carpinus betulus*)
Turkish hazel (*Corylus colurna*)
Hungarian oak (*Quercus frainetto*)
Lime (*Tilia species* and cultivars)
Indian horse chestnut (*Aesculus indica*)
Beech (*Fagus sylvatica*)
Walnut (*Juglans species*)
Zelkova 'Village Green'
Holm oak (*Quercus ilex*)

TREES AS SCREEN

Box (*Buxus sempervirens*)
Tree privet (*Ligustrum lucidum*)
Hornbeam (*Carpinus betulus*)
Corsican pine (*Pinus nigra subsp. laricio*)
London plane (*Platanus × hispanica*)
Indian bean tree (*Catalpa bignonioides*)
Western red cedar (*Thuja plicata*)
Holm oak (*Quercus ilex*)
Sweet bay (*Laurus nobilis*)
Portugal laurel (*Prunus lusitanica*)

TREES FOR INDUSTRIAL SITES

Italian alder (*Alnus cordata*)
Ash (*Fraxinus excelsior*)
Pin oak (*Quercus palustris*)
Eucalyptus (Hardy *species*)
Silver birch (*Betula pendula*)
Grey poplar (*Populus × canescens*)
Swedish whitebeam (*Sorbus intermedia*)
Wingnut (*Pterocarya species*)
Rowan (*Sorbus aucuparia*)
Black locust (*Robinia pseudoacacia*)

TREES FOR WILDLIFE

Field maple (*Acer campestre*)
Holly (*Ilex aquifolium*)
Wayfaring tree (*Viburnum lantana*)
Hawthorn (*Crataegus monogyna*)
Crab apple (*Malus sylvestris*)
Bird cherry (*Prunus padus*)
Wild service tree (*Sorbus torminalis*)
Yew (*Taxus baccata*)
Buckthorn (*Rhamnus cathartica*)
Goat willow (*Salix caprea & hybrids*)

Top: Black locust has a light and airy feel and is a robust tree ideal for industrial sites.

Left: Common lime has long been a popular choice for avenues.

Street tree planting is usually planned and carried out under the direction of the Highways Agency or county council planning and highways departments, with input from utility providers such as water, gas or cable companies. However, at a local level, town, parish and borough councils do seek the views of interested residents including Tree Wardens. All such dialogue, if it ensures good practice and the well-being of the tree, must be helpful.

Local input is probably most valuable when it draws on experience of past successes or failures with trees in the area. Local people who have been involved in planning new plantings also have an important aftercare role. They are the ones who will spot problems at an early stage and notify the appropriate authority. With permission they may even be able to take on some maintenance work such as watering local street trees in dry periods, or hand weeding so that strimmers and other mechanical tools need not be used so much.

NEW STREET TREE SITES

With new street tree planting the key objective should be to enhance the environment, but avoid any nuisance. Will the stem or crown grow so large that it becomes a liability? Will the roots cause dehydration of the subsoil or, closer to the surface, create an uneven footpath that may become a health and safety issue? Will foliage become so dense that houses become gloomy and street lights, road signs or bus stops are obscured? Trees must never be positioned so that they eventually become a traffic hazard. Access to houses and driveways must not be made unsafe. Planting should take into account the needs of residents and road users and be positioned so that wheelchairs are not likely to be restricted, or

people with disabilities such as impaired vision are not endangered.

Street trees work best as landscape features and filters of dust and pollution where the street is wide and where there are either no buildings or they are set back. Modern conditions and constraints suggest that new large trees should only be planted in wide streets, along purpose-built ring roads or in town squares and pedestrian precincts. In other circumstances, the range of smaller trees should be used to create urban treescapes.

Digging holes through concrete, paving or tarmac is a specialist job that should only be undertaken with the right equipment and expertise. Great care is needed because holes in town streets, even after thorough research and consultation, can still contain unexpected surprises. Modern drain and cable detection devices are probably more helpful than Victorian or Edwardian sewer plans.

Two different views of a small suburban development show the use of large trees to provide shade (left) and smaller, decorative, trees such as rowan (above), to create a varied and attractive environment for the residents.

CHOICE OF STREET TREES

The ideal street tree would be versatile and tolerant of physical abuse. It needs to resist or recover from mindless vandalism or brushes with wayward traffic, and put up with near strangulation when stakes and ties are not loosened soon enough. It must also survive root severance when new cables or drains are subsequently laid. It has to contend with unpredictable soil that is likely to lack much oxygen. It needs to tolerate salt when de-icing occurs and resist whatever dogs and other domestic pets may do to it. Unfortunately the perfect street tree does not exist, but there are still many trees that grow well in Britain's streets.

Where conditions are adequate alongside a road, a number of very good, narrow-crowned forms of familiar species have been produced. Their leaves are fairly small, their flowers and fruit do not attract noxious insects and their ultimate size is not excessive. Tough and fairly 'traffic-proof' are two hornbeams, *Carpinus betulus* 'Fastigiata' and 'Columnaris', a black locust, *Robinia pseudoacacia* 'Bessoniana' and some limes that do not have a serious honeydew problem or kill bees, *Tilia cordata* 'Pyramidalis' and 'Greenspire'. Quite unexpectedly, the neat little Mongolian lime (*Tilia mongolica*) is also proving to be highly resistant to roadside fumes and dust.

For wide streets and precincts there are several excellent well-proportioned feature trees. Recent climate change has made Turkish hazel (*Corylus colurna*) a perfect 'paving' tree. Where the soil is wet, pin oak (*Quercus palustris*) fits the bill. Recommended for good autumn foliage colour and good shape are two outstanding pears *Pyrus communis* 'Beech Hill' and *Pyrus calleryana* 'Chanticleer' as well as a narrow-leaved ash (*Fraxinus angustifolia* 'Raywood').

The best native tree for urban use that retains its environmental value and reliably produces good autumn foliage colour is field maple (*Acer campestre*). Other maples, both requiring much more space, are Norway maple (*Acer platanoides*), which has many cultivated forms, and sycamore (*Acer pseudoplatanus*). Where space is more limited, smaller look-alikes for sycamore are Italian maple (*Acer opalus*) and Balkan maple (*Acer hyrcanum*). Note, however, that sycamore, and its smaller cousins, are susceptible to bark stripping in mid-summer by grey squirrels and should not be planted in places where squirrels are encouraged by local residents.

Where a street or square is wide enough to plant shade trees several evergreen species work very well. Climatic change in Britain means that once-tender holm oak (*Quercus ilex*) and cork oak (*Quercus suber*) will thrive in most cities in the British Isles. Harder to find but worth the search is Turner's oak (*Quercus* × *turneri*) which looks just like a common oak but retains its leaves all winter.

In the right conditions some conifers or even palms may be appropriate. Classic deciduous shade trees include the horse chestnut, but this is a brittle unsafe tree in old age. A better choice is the Indian horse chestnut (*Aesculus indica*) which flowers profusely in late June and saves its conkers until November. Italian alder (*Alnus cordata*) casts a pleasant shade and does not demand a wet site. The classic town shade tree is London plane but its ultimate height of 35 metres (115 feet), a crown spread of more than 20 metres (66 feet) and a stem diameter of over 1 metre (3 feet) rule it out for all but the widest city streets.

Opposite: A fine old fastigiate hornbeam in Golden Square in central London.

WHAT SOIL DOES FOR TREES

Natural undisturbed soil is a dynamic living environment composed entirely of rotting plant and animal detritus mixed with the geological material on which it happens to be deposited.

For the tree soil serves three purposes:

- Firstly, it is an anchorage, deep roots holding firmly on to layers of rock or stones.

- Secondly, soil provides the tree with water which is usually taken up as a nutrient-rich solution.

- Thirdly, it provides mineral plant food, notably phosphate, potash and nitrogen.

Supplies of plant food are continually replenished by recycled dead leaves from the tree, other organic plant and animal remains and waste, nitrogen-rich rain water from lightning discharges and mineral salts from the bedrock. All this nutritious material is made available to the tree by fungi and essential micro-organisms living in the soil and essential to its development. This process takes years to develop with the help of worms and invertebrates. Larger animals such as moles, other burrowing animals or birds help to mix and cultivate. Even we can take some credit for soil improvement so long as we appreciate the fragility of the ecosystem.

Most plants live in conditions that range from neutral to slightly acidic. The very process of root growth encourages the development of acidity. Trees will generally survive in acid soil down to pH 4 on a soil testing kit. Clay soils are often around neutral on the pH scale, although wet clays may be acidic and dry clays may be slightly alkaline depending on the origin of the clay (e.g. marl).

Except for possible instability, clays are good for trees. Alkaline soils may cause problems except for species adapted to lime-rich conditions. These soils mostly overlay chalk or limestone. Lime-rich soils can induce chlorosis, an iron deficiency that causes leaf yellowing and stunted growth. However, trees have the ability to adapt to most soil types. Where the natural layers (horizons) in soil have different levels of alkalinity, roots tend to pick the level best suited to their needs. Beech, for example, prefers acid conditions and yet is common in the chalk landscape of southern England, because it feeds in the upper, more acid, soil levels.

Soil evolves continuously. It starts as a film of algae over bare rock, then organic material collects in crevices and cracks until there is enough to support plant roots. Trees such as dwarf willow, rowan, juniper and mountain pine cling to alpine rocks and feed on this young soil. Over thousands of years structure and fauna develop to a highly sophisticated state, resulting in what gardeners call loam. Where the bedrock is acid (e.g. granite) and there is high rainfall, vegetation fails to rot completely and peat is formed. This may eventually be many metres deep and the surface may then be completely cut off from the supply of minerals in the bedrock below.

Much urban tree planting is not on natural soil, but on re-formed or cultivated land, much of it devoid of life. Disturbing soil, even by digging it over, can be retrogressive in soil evolution terms. Natural development is reversed and rainwater charged with carbon dioxide starts to decompose exposed rock minerals into oxides and the whole process starts again. On disturbed ground, so long as some old 'living' soil remains and toxicity is not excessive, trees will grow. Alder, for example, can survive in only 20% of proper soil in a mass of bricks and rubble.

SOIL TYPES

PREPARING THE SOIL FOR PLANTING

For most trees the type of soil is only of limited importance. Only species that insist on acid conditions (e.g. Arbutus, silver fir, Pieris and Rhododendron) will fail completely when planted in the wrong place. Even trees that prefer acidity will usually put up with neutral conditions, but their performance and possibly leaf colour will be less than perfect. English oak, for example, does best in terms of size and timber quality on a moderately acid site but it can be found growing just about anywhere. Drainage may be required on wet soils to improve stability, and cultivation to relieve compaction may improve survival rates. Fertiliser is seldom needed at the time of planting.

MATURE SOIL

With mature soil attention needs only to be paid to drainage, particularly on clay land. Soil compaction at lower levels may need breaking up. Anyone fortunate enough to have a site showing signs of ridges and furrows should cherish it and plant only on the upper two thirds of the ridge. If the surface colour is dark brown the organic content is probably about right and if worms abound fertility is likely to be sufficient. Old woody roots may need to be removed from the planting hole, particularly if nearby trees are showing signs of disease. Every effort should be made to preserve the wildlife living in the soil. Never dig holes too far in advance and allow the soil to dry out.

FORMER ARABLE LAND

Farmland is generally good for most tree planting, especially field margins and corners where there is likely to have been less compaction and fertiliser enrichment. The soil is likely to have developed a 'plough pan', a hard layer just below cultivation level. This needs to be exposed at the bottom of the planting hole and broken up with a fork. Many really ancient and solid plough pans, consolidated by years of traditional tilling, have now been broken up by modern deeper cultivation with powerful tractors and more efficient machinery. The best soil is likely to be where legumes have been recently grown, since they will have enriched soil nitrogen levels and the benefit will pass on to tree roots.

FORMER HEATHLAND

Light sandy soils, often former heathland, are generally hungry and often impoverished. On many sites an 'iron-pan' will have developed, a solid metallic barrier in the sand usually between 30 and 60 cm (12 and 24 inches) deep. It must be broken up in the planting hole. Existing ground vegetation will give clues to impoverished soil: for example, the presence of heather suggests lack of phosphate. Except where the iron pan is solid, drainage is unlikely to be a problem, but drying out is more likely. Choice of species is critical, birch being an obvious candidate.

MOORLAND

Exposure is often a greater problem than soil type on moorland, where soils are mostly peaty, acidic and wet. Restricted drainage leads to 'gleying' where plant roots use up meagre supplies of available oxygen and anaerobic conditions are produced. Grey (ferric oxide) and brown (ferrous oxide) patches in the clay indicate this. It is bad for trees but can be alleviated by thorough deep cultivation.

RE-FORMED LAND

This is widely variable, ranging from builders' rubbish in the garden to a capped landfill site. Suitable types of tree can be determined only when the ground is thoroughly investigated. If there are traces of good soil the prospects are favourable. Dangers are excess acidity, alkalinity, builders' waste such as lime mortar or unseen toxicity. A good sign is a healthy crop of weeds. Nettles, in particular, indicate good fertility. On the poorest sites alders are generally planted as a pioneer crop. Once established, they process nitrogen from the atmosphere and soon improve a bad site with organic leaf litter.

Silver birch, perhaps the best coloniser of all, is equally at home on heathland, moorland or re-formed land.

TREES FOR SOIL TYPES

Common ash thrives on former arable land and will grow fast to become either fine individual specimen trees or, grown in close proximity, will provide a useful crop of long, straight timber.

KEY

***	Very best choice
**	A good choice, but may get very large or develop suckers
*	May require shelter and warmth. May be susceptible to disease or animal damage.

MATURE SOIL
(large amenity trees)

Indian horse chestnut (Aesculus indica) ***

Common oak (Quercus robur) ***

Turkish hazel (Corylus colurna) ***

Algerian oak (Quercus canariensis) ***

Tulip tree (Liriodendron tulipifera) ***

Pagoda tree (Sophora japonica) ***

Silver pendant lime (Tilia tomentosa 'Petiolaris') ***

London plane (Platanus × hispanica) **

Oriental plane (Platanus orientalis) **

Black walnut (Juglans nigra) *

MATURE SOIL
(small trees)

Field maple (Acer campestre) ***

Sweet birch (Betula lenta) ***

Honey locust (Gleditsia triacanthos) ***

Yellow-wood (Cladrastis kentukea) Syn. C. lutea ***

Double wild cherry (Prunus avium 'Plena') ***

Sargent's cherry (Prunus sargentii) *

Tupelo (Nyssa sylvatica) *

Lace-bark pine (Pinus bungeana) *

Tibetan cherry (Prunus serrula) *

Sweet gum (Liquidambar stryaciflua) *

FORMER ARABLE LAND
(farm woodland trees)

Italian alder (Alnus cordata) ***

American ash (Fraxinus americana) ***

Common ash (Fraxinus excelsior) ***

Silver maple (Acer saccharinum) **

Tree of Heaven (Ailanthus altissima) **

Beech (Fagus sylvatica) *

Black walnut (Juglans nigra) *

Walnut (Juglans regia) *

Southern beech (Nothofagus nervosa) *

Sycamore (Acer pseudoplatanus) *

Left: The tulip tree is a splendid amenity tree, seen here at its autumnal best.

Below left: Autumn leaves of silver maple, a good choice for former arable land.

Below right: The field maple is an excellent smaller species for mature soils.

Right: Norway maple is an ideal species for heavy clay soils.

Below left: Common juniper is well-suited to heathland.

Below right: Elder, not always a popular choice with tree planters and frequently regarded as a weed, is a remarkably useful tree for its flowers, fruit and bark, and tends to thrive on re-formed land.

HEAVY CLAY SOILS

Ash *(Fraxinus excelsior)* ***
Plane *(Platanus species)* ***
Lime *(Tilia species)* ***
Norway maple *(Acer platanoides)* ***
Pin oak *(Quercus palustris)* ***
Holly *(Ilex aquifolium)* ***
Wayfaring tree *(Viburnum lantana)* ***
Alder *(Alnus species)* ***
Eucalyptus (Hardy *species)* **
Black locust *(Robinia pseudoacacia)* **

FORMER HEATHLAND

Silver birch *(Betula pendula)* ***
Red alder *(Alnus rubra)* ***
Blackthorn *(Prunus spinosa)* ***
Rowan *(Sorbus aucuparia)* ***
Common juniper *(Juniperus communis)* ***
Pine *(Pinus species)* ***
Arizona cypress *(Cupressus glabra)* ***
Sea buckthorn *(Hippophae rhamnoides)* **
White poplar *(Populus alba)* **
Dogwood *(Cornus sanguinea)* *

Larch is likely to grow very well on former moorland.

RE-FORMED LAND

Grey alder *(Alnus incana)* ***
White poplar *(Populus alba)* ***
Pin oak *(Quercus palustris)* ***
Rowan *(Sorbus aucaparia)* ***
Elder *(Sambucus nigra)* ***
Common alder *(Alnus glutinosa)* ***
Birch *(Betula species)* ***
Black locust *(Robinia pseudoacacia)* **
Tree of Heaven *(Ailanthus altissima)* **
Wingnut *(Pterocarya species)* **

FORMER MOORLAND

Silver birch *(Betula pendula)* ***
Hairy birch *(Betula pubescens)* ***
Swedish whitebeam *(Sorbus intermedia)* ***
Silver fir *(Abies species)* ***
Spruce *(Picea species)* ***
Sessile oak *(Quercus petraea)* ***
Larch *(Larix species)* ***
Grey poplar *(Populus × canescens)* **
Aspen *(Populus tremula)* **
River birch *(Betula nigra)* *

An established tree affects soil in two ways: by modifying the nutrient cycle and water availability. The consequences for competing plant life will vary according to whether the tree is growing in a flower bed or in grass.

Trees planted into concrete or tarmac are more or less restricted to simply improving the underlying soil by drying it up a little and, where there is sufficient oxygen, filling it with surface roots, some of which may eventually cause surface irregularities.

Nutrients and minerals are recycled from the subsoil by deep tree roots and distributed on the surface in the form of dead leaves. These are soon pulled directly into the ground by worms and other organisms; or else they provide surface mulch which rots down into a rich organic layer of debris.

Tidy gardeners can of course sweep up all the leaves and compost them elsewhere, but it is sensible to put the end product back in order to maintain the health and fertility of the soil. If dead leaves are continually removed, soil structure will eventually deteriorate until tree and other plant growth will be unsustainable without top-up applications of fertiliser and imported soil ameliorants. Deciduous trees produce a rapid turnover of nutrients but evergreens also drop their leaves, over a protracted period.

Water circulation in soil changes after a tree is established. Excess ground moisture in spring is absorbed, reducing the damage of run-off or water-logging while the soil is still cold after the winter. This is a critical time for surface rooting plants on heavy soils, so perennials growing close to a tree will benefit. The reduction of cold water in upper layers of the soil allows accelerated warming which is essential for growth.

Later on, trees shade the earth from the summer sun. At this time of year, when in many areas soil moisture is in short supply, trees take the bulk of their water from deep in the ground and do not compete directly with herbaceous plants or grasses.

The beneficial effects of shading and wind reduction enable most plants growing under most trees to contend with drought conditions rather better than they would in the open. One exception to this is the barrier to summer rain imposed by tree foliage. Beech, in particular, can hold back all the rain in a light summer shower.

None of it reaches the ground even for the benefit of the tree itself because it evaporates immediately. Mulching with fallen leaves can also deprive the topsoil of moisture if it is done artificially in spring or summer. In the autumn, however, mulching will soon be soaked by winter rain and the effect is reversed. It becomes resistant to drying out and keeps the topsoil moist.

Tree roots bind soil together so that it is less vulnerable to erosion, especially on steep slopes or close to running water. When a tree dies or is felled the root system slowly rots down, leaving a moist labyrinth of humus-rich tunnels running deep into the earth. These provide an easy path for the roots of future trees to follow provided that they do not contain pathogens such as honey fungus.

Fallen leaves can provide a useful source of nutrients and minerals.

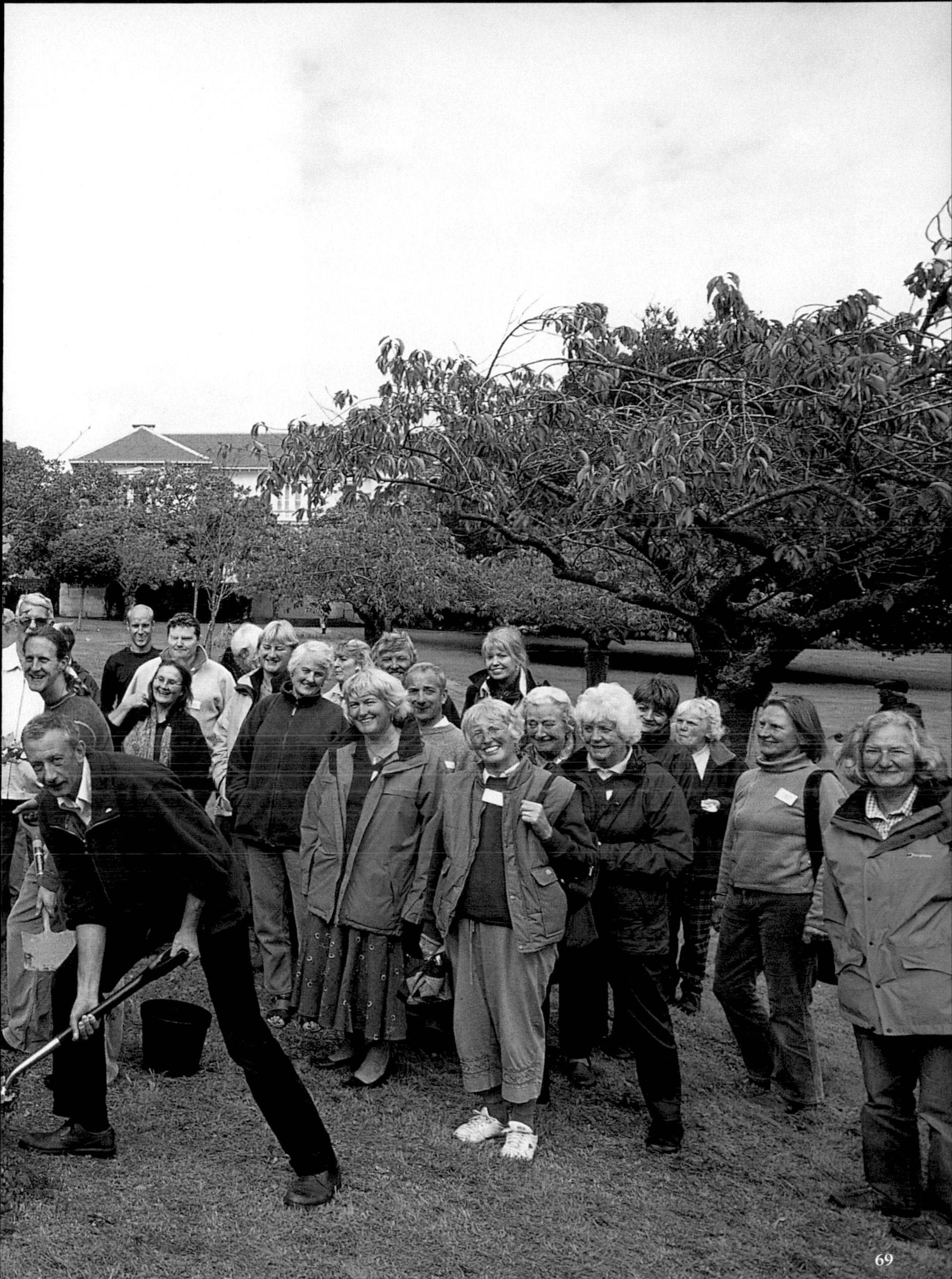

Container-grown trees are ideal for planting at any time of year.

Once a tree has been chosen for 'your ground' it is essential to give it the best possible start in life. Here are some practical tips to help maximise its chances of growing to maturity.

WHEN TO PLANT

Trees with bare roots should only be planted between November and March – when they are dormant – and preferably not when the ground is frozen. Hard frost is most likely in January and February. Half-hardy species (suitable only for western coastal districts) should be planted in spring.

Trees grown in containers can be planted at any time of year, but the following guidelines will give best results for them too. If, however, they are planted in late spring or summer, they should be watered during dry spells in the first growing season.

The best time to plant bare-root trees is between November and March.

- A good time to plant trees is during The Tree Council's National Tree Week, which starts at the end of November and continues until the first Sunday in December.

- For deciduous trees, it is best to plant before Christmas. Although they will probably survive spring planting, they are more likely to suffer from drought than if planted in the autumn or early winter.

- For evergreens, early or late in the planting season are the best times. If planting in spring, wait until the soil has begun to warm and the first flush of new growth occurs.

- In dry areas, late autumn planting is best for most species as this gives trees a chance to become established before spring droughts.

- In wet areas, early spring planting is generally best. Ideally, excess water should first be drained from the site because if wet soils freeze there is a risk of 'frost lift' which can devastate newly planted trees. This is unlikely to happen in most years, especially if a hedge protects the site.

Whenever the trees are planted the roots should be shaded, cool and damp. It is also important to firm in the trees by treading in well.

WHERE TO PLANT

There are many places where it is possible to plant trees – with the owner's permission. Here are some of the options:

- Front and back gardens
- Existing tree pits in streets
- Roundabouts
- Grass verges
- Traffic islands
- Social housing land
- Parks and open spaces
- School/college grounds
- Nature reserves and woodlands (do not disturb the ecological balance)
- Golf courses
- Hospital grounds
- Industrial estates
- Office car parks
- Areas around shops
- Playing fields
- Derelict land and development sites
- City farms and community gardens

The environment around hospitals, when planted with trees, has been shown to be beneficial to the well-being and recovery of patients

Vast open spaces of car parks are made more visually appealing by planting trees.

Tree planting around offices and on industrial estates makes a greener, more pleasant environment in which to work.

LANDSCAPE AND LEGAL CONSIDERATIONS

Once the potential site has been selected, other factors need to be considered:

- **Consent.** Trees may only be planted with the landowner's permission.

- **The proximity of buildings and other structures.** Trees close to buildings and other structures may cause damage either directly (e.g. to boundary walls or paving) or indirectly (e.g. tree related subsidence to low rise buildings).

- **Architectural setting.** The tree form and colour should complement the surrounding built environment.

- **The context of the broader landscape.** Trees should match the soft or hard landscape features amongst which they will be planted.

- **Possible problems a tree may cause in a particular situation.** Ultimate size may create unwelcome shade, or the tree may come into contact with buildings and windows.

- **Overhead services.** As they grow, trees may interfere with overhead electric cables or phone wires, and will therefore require constant pruning to prevent damage to the services. Avoid planting in these circumstances.

- **Underground services.** If underground cables are suspected, contact the tree officer without delay. Apart from the possible risk of serious harm to the person digging in such areas (i.e. over electric and gas services), the services themselves may be damaged, incurring significant repair costs. In any event subsequent renewal or maintenance of the services will result in problems for the overlying tree.

- **Road sight lines or road signs.** Trees which block sight lines, for instance at road junctions and bends, can prove hazardous to road users and pedestrians.

- **Street or security lighting.** Blocking of light by trees at night can have obvious implications for safety.

Young trees are on sale in a variety of forms. They can be:

- **Container-grown:** as the container protects the roots, these trees can be planted at any season but they are more expensive, require good care and may need plenty of water if the first season after planting is dry.
- **Bare-rooted:** acceptable for most deciduous species provided they are planted outside the growing season
- **Root-balled:** for evergreen and exotic species

Trees are also available in different sizes – known as transplant, whip, feathered, standard and heavy standard. However whips are cheaper, easy to move and usually establish better than larger trees.

If buying trees from a nursery, check the origin of each species and be wary if the nursery is unable to supply the information: some give it in their catalogues. Many now have a policy of increasing the use of seed from British sources.

It is worth considering planting trees which have been raised from the seed of healthy trees growing on or near the site to be planted. This helps to ensure the survival of local genetic strains.

Before buying a tree, check that it is healthy and undamaged, and that its roots are moist and not 'pot-bound'. Do not buy trees, or return them immediately to the nursery, if they look unfit for planting.

OBTAINING TREES

Local suppliers of trees – listed, for example, in the The Yellow Pages under 'Nurseries-Horticultural' or 'Garden Centres' – are mostly likely to specialise in container-grown ornamental stock. However, many garden centres will supply other types of tree to order.

To get hold of native trees in quantity, a good starting point is to contact the local Wildlife Trust or BTCV office, or even the tree officer at the county or district council, who should be able to provide the names of local suppliers.

If large numbers of trees are required, it is best to place orders as early as possible – by July or August for supply in the late autumn/winter – and specify a delivery date. However, be prepared to be flexible on when the delivery actually takes place because mild or very wet weather can affect when the stock can be lifted, just as very cold weather can delay planting. Bare-rooted trees will only be lifted when the plants are dormant. The dormant period usually starts in October/November, but it depends on the species concerned and the weather. If it is mild late into the autumn, lifting will have to be delayed.

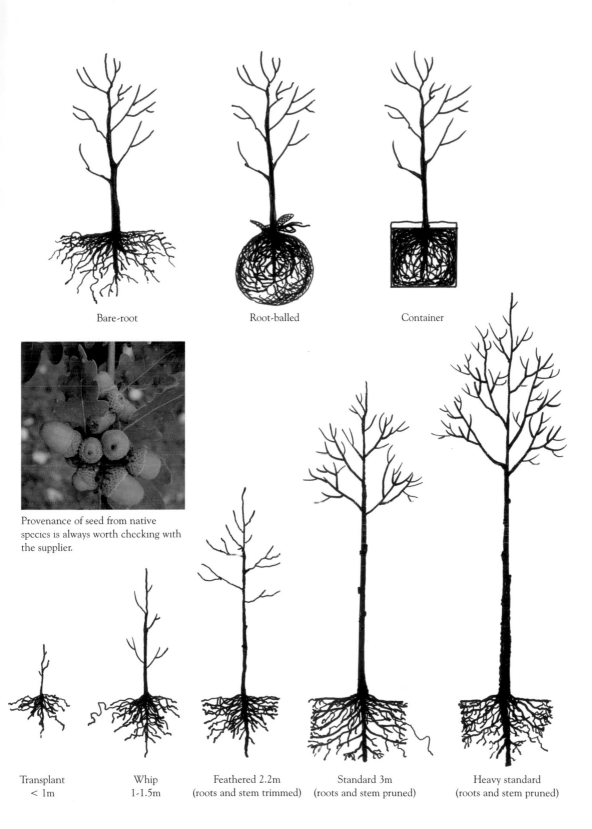

Bare-root

Root-balled

Container

Provenance of seed from native species is always worth checking with the supplier.

Transplant
< 1m

Whip
1-1.5m

Feathered 2.2m
(roots and stem trimmed)

Standard 3m
(roots and stem pruned)

Heavy standard
(roots and stem pruned)

Opposite: A superb selection of container-grown trees in a nursery.

Because of careless handling between the time trees are lifted from the nursery and when they are finally planted out, thousands of them each year turn out to be already dead when they are planted. Unfortunately this is not easy to spot before the trees are planted and the first sign of a problem may be when they fail to grow.

To minimise the risk it is essential to ensure that:

- ■ trees are stored only where there is free drainage, so that they do not stand in waterlogged conditions

- ■ the roots are protected from heat

- ■ bare root trees are delivered with their roots wrapped in plastic and only stored for a maximum of 24 hours, making sure they are in a cool shady position out of the wind

- ■ if not planted immediately, bare-root trees are removed from the bags and heeled-in (see opposite)

- ■ root-balled and container-grown trees are stored upright, standing on an impervious surface

- ■ as much short fibrous root is kept on the trees as possible

- ■ mechanical damage, such as broken stem tops or bark stripped from stem or roots, is avoided

Retain as much fibrous root as possible and avoid damage.

Broken branches and insufficient roots should be avoided.

Store trees in a bag, in the shade with tops kept free.

Do not store in water.

HEELING-IN

Ideally, trees should be lifted, transported and replanted without interruption. If, however, they need to be stored before planting the traditional approach is to heel them in.

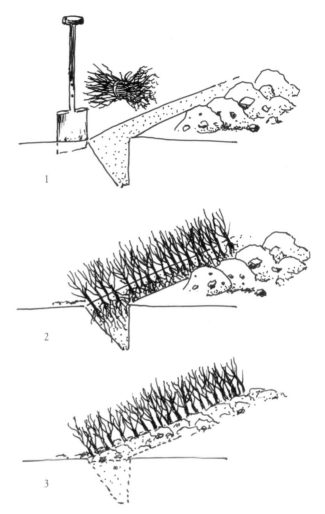

1   Dig a trench in good fresh moist soil which will not dry out or become waterlogged. Cultivated but shaded nursery ground is ideal. Dig the trench with a sloping back, deep enough for the trees to be put in and their roots completely covered.

2   Separate trees into bundles and space them along the trench to keep those in the centres of the bundles from drying out or – in the case of evergreens – from heating up. Place the trees with their roots completely in the trench but with their branches out.

3   Cover the roots with soil and lightly firm it around the roots by treading it in.

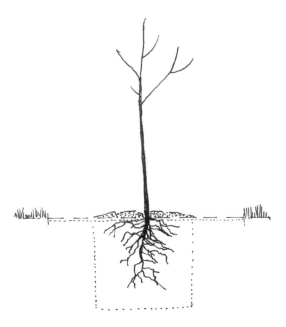

Good soil: plant tree in a hole large enough for roots to be spread out. Clear grass 1 metre (3 feet) diameter around tree and slightly over-fill the hole.

PREPARING THE PLANTING HOLE OR PIT

Newly planted trees must have plenty of room for their roots to give them the best possible start.

- In good quality soil, dig a hole or pit large enough for all the roots to be spread out.

- In poor soil, dig a hole wider and deeper than is needed to accommodate the roots and partly refill it with the soil that has been removed. Before doing this, break up the compacted soil in and around it to improve drainage and aeration of the roots.

- After putting the tree in the pit, start filling around the roots, treading increasingly firmly until the hole is over-filled and leaving the soil slightly above the surrounding ground level. Treading in is most important when pit planting. Many failures are due to lack of firming. In heavy soils do not firm so much that the soil becomes compacted.

- Clear grass and weeds for a space of 1 metre (3 feet) diameter around the tree so that they do not compete with it for moisture.

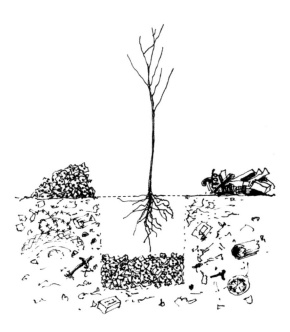

Poor soil: plant tree in a larger hole, remove all rubble, and break up compacted soil. If possible, fill hole with better quality soil.

STAKES AND OTHER SUPPORTS

Stakes and other supports are necessary only if a new tree is more than 1 metre (3 feet) tall and only for its first year. After this, a well-planted tree should no longer need support.

- If a stake is necessary, attach the tree to it using a flexible tie which will stretch as the tree grows.

- Loosen or remove the tie if it appears to be strangling the tree at any time.

TREE SHELTERS

Shelters are put around young trees to prevent animals – from mice and rabbits to deer, sheep, cattle and horses – eating the leaves or stripping the bark and so damaging the tree.

Check shelters in spring and autumn to ensure they are effective (no bark missing or twigs bitten or broken off) and not rubbing or cutting into the tree.

- If a shelter is not fulfilling its purpose, add more protection, e.g. a taller tree shelter to protect against animals

- Replace/repair damaged shelters

- If a shelter is damaging the tree, adjust, modify or replace it

- If the threat no longer exists because the tree has grown or circumstances have changed remove the shelter so that there is no risk of damage to the tree

Different types of tree shelters (from the top):
cage, spiral, square and round tubes.

- Soak the roots with water for a few hours before planting

- Dig a hole for the tree that is large enough to allow its roots to be spread out

- Prune any damaged twigs

- Remove any containers and if necessary tease out any 'pot-bound' roots and remove any damaged ones

- When planting bare-root trees, space the roots out carefully, having made the hole big enough to avoid bending any roots

- Carefully hold the tree upright in the middle of the hole, while putting soil over the roots in thin layers

- Insert a stake into the hole if required – not needed for trees less than 1 metre (3 feet) tall – ensuring no roots are damaged

- Shake the tree gently up and down so that the soil gets between and around the roots, and firm the soil with your foot

- Continue filling around the roots, treading more firmly until the hole is over-filled, leaving the soil slightly above the surrounding ground. Ensure that when planting is completed the root collar will be level with the ground surface

- If a support is being used, secure the tree to it with a flexible tie

- If the soil is dry, water well

- Apply mulch around the tree – bark or composted woody material, a mulch mat or cut up squares of carpet. Add an adequate shelter if there is a risk of damage from animals or machines

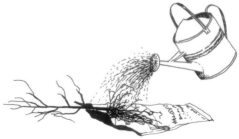

Moisten roots (but do not wash all the soil off).

Dig hole, removing roots and rubbish
(not more than half a day before planting).

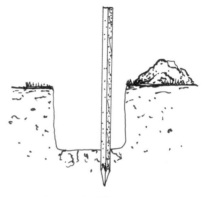

Insert stake (if necessary).

Mix organic material or soil improver,
with spoil, if required.

Fill hole and firm up.

Root and shoot prune.

Fix tie, mulch mat, mulch, guard
(and label) and water in.

Part fill hole, position plant with root collar
level with surface of ground.

It is not sufficient just to plant a tree well. Even when it has finally been planted in its new site, it will continue to need regular attention to help it thrive during the critical early years.

Far too many newly planted trees die in the first five years due, in part, to a lack of aftercare. The Tree Council's Trees Love Care (TLC) Campaign highlights the three simple tasks that need to be carried out at least once a year for the first five years to ensure that the young tree survives and thrives. TLC for young trees involves:

> **T**ending, such as checking shelters and carrying out essential pruning to remove broken and dead branches
>
> **L**oosening ties and checking stakes
>
> **C**learing all weeds and grasses, ideally from one metre square (3 feet diameter) around the base of each tree, and applying mulch

TENDING

Check the tree in March or April every year.

- Is it alive? If there are no leaves, look for green under the bark of twigs (scrape the surface with a fingernail or knife) and living buds

- Fill in any gaps in the soil around the roots and use a foot to firm the new soil. Also if the soil has been lifted by frost, firm it down

- If the soil is waterlogged, channel/drain the excess water away from the tree

- Look for damage caused by pests and diseases

- If the tree is dead, try to work out why and correct the problem (seeking advice if necessary) before planting a new one

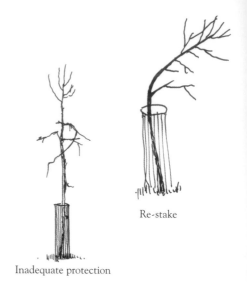

Re-stake

Inadequate protection

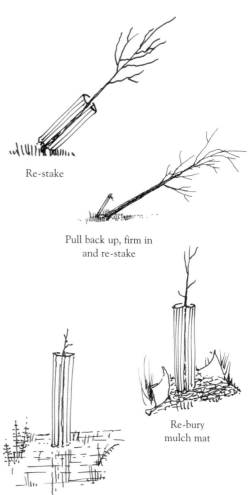

Re-stake

Pull back up, firm in and re-stake

Re-bury mulch mat

Drain

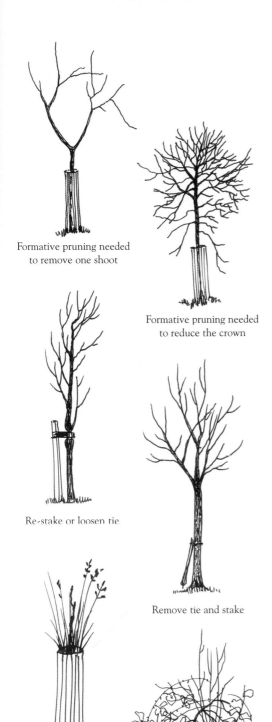

Formative pruning needed
to remove one shoot

Formative pruning needed
to reduce the crown

Re-stake or loosen tie

Remove tie and stake

Weed problem

Clear weeds to
reduce competition

PRUNING

Careful formative pruning can prevent problems in later life. If a tree has two competing upright shoots, remove one at an early stage to leave a single main shoot. This can save the tree from possible future branch failure.

LOOSENING

- ■ Check the stake and the tie. Is the tie too tight? The tree stem should not be under pressure from the tie, and should not rub against the stake or tree shelter

- ■ Does the tree still need a stake? A young tree should only need one until its roots have grown into undisturbed soil to give it stability, which generally takes a year. Check this in spring by releasing the tie and if the tree stays upright, remove the stake

- ■ If the tree leans and the roots move or if it is top heavy and bends over, shorten the stake (to just above the bend, if relevant) and replace the tie at the top of the stake to ensure the stem stands upright

CLEARING

- ■ Pull up or hoe any grass and weeds for a radius of at least 0.5 metres (1.5 feet) around the tree. Take care to avoid damage to the tree's roots

- ■ Early in the year, when the soil is moist, cover the cleared area with a mulch mat, bark or brushwood chippings, or old piece of carpet. This helps retain moisture near the roots, reduces competition from weeds, and means there is no need to use grass-cutting machinery near the tree where it might damage the bark

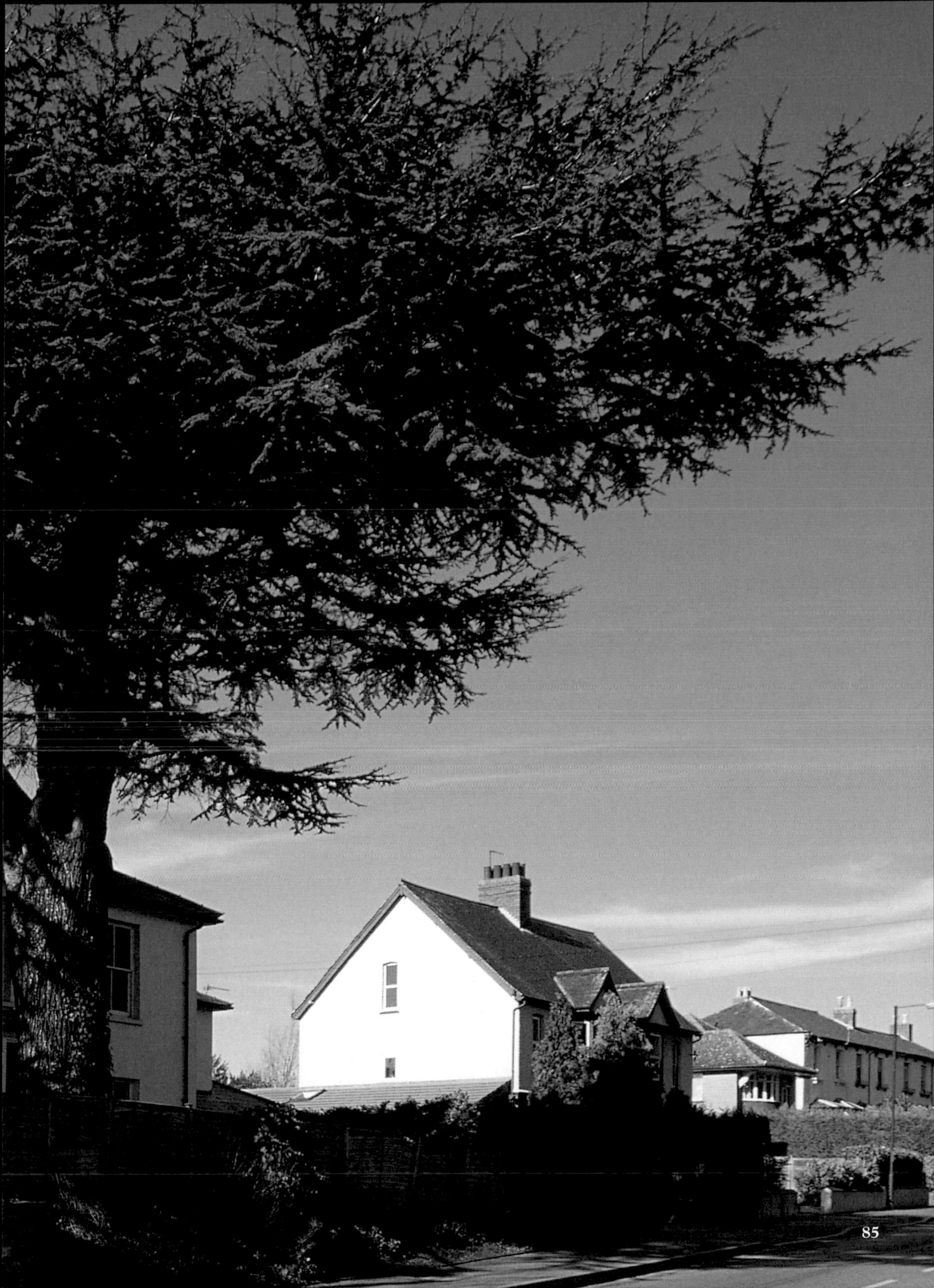

Even well-intentioned tree planting may raise eyebrows or be in conflict with the interests of others, although few involved in planting schemes plan to break the law. It is important, therefore, that tree planting is carefully planned.

On your own land you can plant what you want, where you want, provided the growing tree does not damage third parties and their property. A tree planted close to a boundary is likely to overhang it, which may be a nuisance, but does not in itself constitute an infringement of the neighbour's property. Nevertheless, it may be prudent, before buying a tree, to consider the likely branch spread at maturity. The alternative is to be prepared to get rid of the developing tree after some years but before legal conflicts arise. Such a strategy, carried out rigorously, should be acceptable provided another tree is planted as a replacement.

It is essential to gain the owner's permission when trees are to be planted on someone else's land. That applies equally to publicly- and privately-owned land. Under the Highways Acts it is necessary to obtain a licence from the Highways Authority before planting along a roadside. Responsibility for any trees planted under licence will normally rest with the Highways Authority, but make sure that responsibility is accepted.

With time a tree's trunk can affect users of adjoining properties even when branches do not overhang the boundary.

Many householders object not only to loss of light, but also loss of a view, and loss of television reception. There is no legal right to a view across the land of a third party; similarly there is no legal right to receive television signals across somebody else's land. Nevertheless, such potential conflicts should be considered when judging the suitability of a location for tree planting.

Not everybody loves trees. Those who dislike trees complain about falling leaves and twigs, fruit and other debris (e.g. bird droppings and honeydew). While so far there have not been any successful prosecutions of a tree owner for debris falling from a tree, it is sensible to try to avoid disputes. For example, large-leaved trees cause more problems than those with small leaves; large, hard and fleshy fruits are more likely to generate concerns than small wind-blown seeds.

Roots cause the most expensive and, arguably, the most acrimonious conflicts between property owners, and with any other interest there may be in the land on which a tree grows. In tree care and management there is no greater cause of conflicts, resulting in the loss of many trees – often unnecessarily.

All potentials for conflict and antagonism to trees must be taken seriously because they can generate so much animosity that future tree planting will be threatened, if not prevented. Each opportunity for planting should be regarded as a significant challenge, but careful selection from the vast array of species and cultivars available in Britain should cut disputes to a minimum.

Trees on adjoining properties have often been the cause of contentious issues, such as: ownership, overshadowing, loss of view, root damage and risks of windfall damage.

Tree roots develop in soil to absorb water to sustain the leaves and general physiological functions of the tree. They provide anchorage to withstand strong winds and they also store carbohydrates needed for future growth.

A popular misconception is that different trees species have particular root systems – either deep or shallow. This may be true in ideal soil conditions, but rarely, if ever, do trees have such a luxury. Soil conditions dictate where roots can grow. Oxygen becomes less available with depth, and rain water may be used by herbaceous plants before it reaches tree roots deep in the soil. Increasing depth of soil is accompanied by increasing soil density, making water and root penetration more difficult. Water-logging and toxic materials are also problems.

As a result two broad rules can be applied to all trees wherever they are. The majority of roots of any tree will be found in the upper 60cm (2 feet) of soil; roots may spread radially in any direction, often for a distance greater than the height of the tree. The root system of a tree occupies a very shallow but wide volume of soil (similar to a wine glass sitting on a dinner plate).

In spite of this shallow root system there can still be conflict between tree roots and other users of the soil. Roots may damage structures directly or indirectly.

DIRECT DAMAGE

When a root or the base of a trunk grows into contact with a structure, it cannot grow without applying direct pressure. If the structure is not strong enough to withstand the pressure damage will occur. If it is strong the root may be deflected, distort around the obstacle, or simply stop growing and die.

Pressure does not come from the tip of the root pressing against the structure, but is generated as the diameter of the root increases, displacing paving stones and cracking paths, for example. Other common forms of direct damage seen are cracked garden or garage walls that are only a single brick thick. Houses are generally too heavy for roots to 'lift' and so escape such damage.

Cases of direct damage should be assessed and solutions decided in the light of the circumstances.

When planting in new locations, future direct damage will be minimised if the tree can be planted 2 to 3 metres (6 to 10 feet) from vulnerable structures.

Reduce future problems with footpaths by selecting suitable species and cultural practices.

INDIRECT DAMAGE

Indirect damage to structures occurs when roots extract water from the soil supporting foundations. However, this damage arises only when the soil is shrinkable – its volume changes as its water content alters. Further, the foundations must be unable to accommodate movement that might occur in the supporting soil.

Where the subsoil does not shrink as it dries, there should be no risk of indirect damage from trees close by. The problem should not arise with new buildings because the foundations should have been designed and built to take account of the subsoil's characteristics.

Buildings on shrinkable clay may have foundations that can accommodate any movement in the supporting soil. If there is no information about the subsoil or the foundations, the safe position for a new planting would be a distance from the structure matching the expected mature height of the tree.

Root damage to a pavement from this birch tree is clearly discernible and the group of Tree Wardens (inset picture) show the extent of the problem.

New trees have to be planted, but all too frequently that is regarded as the end of the task. As a result many young trees fail to become established and remain as evidence of poor cultural practices. Blame for the failure is often inappropriately assigned to some insect pest or, more commonly, a disease.

Insect pests rarely afflict young trees in sufficient quantity to threaten their survival, though an exception might be bark beetles colonising pine trees planted as container-grown specimens more than 1 to 1.5 metres (3 to 5 feet) tall. Greater threats are mammals such as voles, rabbits and hares that can eat foliage or strip bark from the stem and roots. Timely protection or weed control should remove the threat.

Fungal and bacterial diseases pose a greater threat to young trees. These organisms affect young and old trees alike. However some, such as fungi causing decay, are more common on mature or over-mature trees. Nevertheless, there have been instances of young trees killed by honey fungus spreading from infected woody material in the soil. Conversely some diseases are a serious threat to young trees, but have little effect on mature ones. This is because of the differences in the tree's size. A fungus infecting a branch or stem of a young tree can quickly cause fatal girdling while in mature trees there are more shoots and they have connections to much larger branches and trunks.

Among the most damaging threats are the Nectria species (for example Coral spot) and Stereum species which affect twigs and shoots by invading through wounds or dead tissue. Soil-borne fungi such as Phytophthora and Vericillium species can also prove devastating to young trees.

However, many trees die simply because they are unable to become established. This can result from poor plant handling between the nursery and planting. Other dangers are inappropriate soil conditions for healthy root activity: these should have been corrected before planting.

After planting, trees are very vulnerable to water stress – too much or too little. The instinctive response to browning leaves is to irrigate, but does the tree need water? Will the water reach the roots or will herbaceous plants around the tree intercept the water? Research has shown that weed control to create weed-free conditions at least 1 metre (3 feet) diameter around each tree will do much to ensure the tree is not threatened by an inadequate water supply.

Attention to detail and thorough planning followed by a little regular tender loving care should minimise the risk of newly planted trees failing to become established.

Typical manifestations of coral spot
(left) and phytopthora (below).

Opposite: an apple tree killed by honey fungus (above), first
showed signs of stress only two years before its final demise.

If trees or shrubs are to be planted near electricity cables or gas pipelines, the type of tree or shrub and its planting must be considered to avoid root damage to buried mains or services. Damage to trees or shrubs from subsequent excavations for repair and maintenance will also be avoided if any planting is carefully positioned or roots are prevented from encroaching on to the services. Planting schemes should be submitted to National Grid or the appropriate utility for approval.

National Grid is required by law to record the location of electricity cables, gas mains, plant and other equipment that may be found in streets. Anyone carrying out excavations is legally required to request and use these records during the works.

UNDERGROUND ELECTRICITY CABLES

Underground electricity cables are normally buried in the ground about 1 metre (3 feet) below the surface. In towns and cities National Grid's cables may be found in roads, pavements, canal tow paths and parks.

The impact of tree roots on underground electricity cables can be significant:

- Where tree roots are entangled with cables, those cables may be disturbed and damaged if the tree falls, cutting off power to customers

- Tree roots alter soil moisture. A cable's rating relies heavily on the environment, especially the thermal resitivity (TR) value of the soil. The TR value usually, but not always, depends on the moisture in the soil. The higher the moisture content the better the TR value. If trees or bushes take up some of the soil's natural moisture this will make the TR value worse and reduce the rating of the cable

- Maintaining and replacing high voltage underground cables requires excavation of the ground. This can be extremely difficult if tree roots surround the cable

Trees should not be planted directly over or within 3 metres (10 feet) of a National Grid high voltage underground electricity cable.

When considering tree species in the vicinity of underground services choose varieties that do not have deep root systems. Also consider the use of root restraints to prevent encroachment on to services.

If excavating or planning to plant a tree within 5 metres (16 feet) of a National Grid high voltage electricity cable, remember to contact National Grid's Transmission Enquiry team first on 0800 731 2961. Always dial before you dig.

GAS PIPELINES

- Before planting any tree on a pipeline easement written approval should be obtained from National Grid.

- The written consent to plant trees should state what area may be planted and also the type of tree.

- Poplar and willow trees should not be planted within 10 metres (33 feet) of the pipeline.

- The following trees must not be planted within 6 metres (20 feet) of the pipeline: ash, cedar, larch, beech, elm, horse chestnut, sweet chestnut, London plane, hornbeam, lime, lime alder, scots pine, black pine, oak, sycamore, apple, plum, cherry, pear and

Trees should not be planted near gas pipelines, to ensure their roots don't damage the pipes.

most conifers. These trees should only be planted as individual specimens or a single row at a distance of between 6 and 10 metres (20 to 33 feet) of the pipeline. Dense mass planting should only be carried out at a distance greater than 10 metres (33 feet) from the pipeline.

■ Raspberries, loganberries, gooseberries and currants may be planted on the easement but a 3 metre (10 feet) strip centred on the pipeline should be left clear at all times except in places where planting is required, for surface stabilisation.

■ Apple trees grafted on to dwarf root stocks may be planted to within 3 metres (10 feet) of the pipeline.

■ In cases where screening is required, the following shallow rooting varieties may be planted over the pipeline, road and field crossings where necessary: blackthorn, broom, cotoneaster, elder, hazel, laurel, privet, quickthorn, snowberry and most ornamental shrubs.

■ Christmas trees (Picea abies) may be planted to within 3 metres (10 feet) of the pipeline. However, permission is given on the strict understanding that the trees are clear-felled at intervals not exceeding seven years.

Environmental charity The Tree Council is a partnership of organisations working together to make trees matter to everyone. It also works towards more trees, of the right kind, in the right places; for better care for all trees, of all ages; and to inspire effective action for trees.

The Tree Council was founded in 1974, with government backing, to keep up the momentum of National Tree Planting Year – Plant a Tree in '73. It is now the UK's lead tree campaigning partnership. Its 150 member organisations range from voluntary, professional, specialist and trade organisations to local authorities and government bodies – all committed to the planting, care, conservation and appreciation of trees.

In 1975 it started National Tree Week, now the UK's largest annual celebration of trees and woods. Over 20 million trees have been planted as a result and millions of people of all ages have been involved, some getting their first taste of why trees matter to their patch. More recently The Tree Council launched three other annual public involvement initiatives: the Trees Love Care campaign (March to September), Walk in the Woods (throughout May), and Seed Gathering Season (September /October).

These were all pioneered by the volunteers who make up the Tree Warden Scheme, which is run in partnership with National Grid and the Office of the Deputy Prime Minister and is key to the success of Trees in Your Ground.

The Tree Council launched the national Scheme in 1990 and now there are many thousands of Tree Wardens championing their communities' trees in local networks covering a third of the British Isles. These networks are co-ordinated by local authorities, voluntary organisations or, increasingly, local partnerships.

Tree Wardens, as well as Tree Council member organisations, play vital roles in the Tree Council's Green Monuments Campaign – a major drive for proper safeguards for heritage trees – and its Hedge Tree Campaign in support of the Government Biodiversity Action Plan.

Through initiatives like these, The Tree Council achieves significant gains in tree cover and greater awareness of how much Trees Matter to everyone's ground.

For further information visit
www.treecouncil.org.uk

NATIONAL GRID

National Grid has worked in partnership with The Tree Council since 1990 and has supported its national Tree Warden Scheme since 1997.

The company has to manage trees and vegetation to ensure the continuity, reliability and safety of its services. The expert advice it receives from The Tree Council, together with the experience of Tree Wardens, is vital in helping it to do this in a safe, sustainable and sympathetic way, and so protect the environment and improve biodiversity for future generations.

ELECTRICITY TRANSMISSION

National Grid owns, maintains and operates the National Electricity Transmission System in England and Wales, and operates the system in Scotland providing electricity supplies from generating stations to local distribution companies. National Grid does not distribute electricity to individual premises, but its role in the wholesale market is key in ensuring a reliable and quality supply to all. The high voltage electricity system, which operates at 400,000 and 275,000 volts, is made up of approximately 22,000 pylons with an overhead line route length of 7000 kilometres (nearly 4500 miles), 660 kilometres (over 400 miles) of underground cable and 341 substations.

GAS TRANSMISSION

In addition, National Grid owns and operates the high-pressure gas transmission system in England, Scotland and Wales, comprising 7000 kilometres (nearly 4500 miles) of high-pressure gas pipeline.

GAS DISTRIBUTION

National Grid is also the local distributor of gas to homes and businesses in many parts of England, including North London, East of England, West Midlands and the North West of England. National Grid is not a supplier of gas, but provides the networks through which it flows in these areas.

For more information about National Grid visit **www.nationalgrid.com**

BOOKS

Here is a selection of the vast range of books on trees, which are considered by the authors to be particularly useful.

Cassell's Trees of Britain and Northern Europe: John White, David Moore (Illustrator)

Collins Tree Guide: Owen Johnson

Field Guide to the Trees of Britain and Europe (Collins Field Guide): Alan Mitchell, P. Dahlstrom (Translator), E. Sunesen (Translator), C. Darter (Translator)

Hillier Gardener's Guide to Trees and Shrubs: John Kelly (Editor)

Hugh Johnson's International Book of Trees: A Guide and Tribute to the Trees of Our Gardens and Forests: Hugh Johnson

The Garden Tree: An Illustrated Guide to Choosing, Planting and Caring for 500 Garden Trees: Alan Mitchell, Allen Coombes

The Tree & Shrub Specialist: The Essential Guide to Selecting, Planting, Improving, and Maintaining Trees and Shrubs in the Garden: David Squire, Alan Bridgewater (Editor), Gill Bridgewater (Editor)

Trees for Small Gardens (RHS Practical Guides): Royal Horticultural Society

Tree Form, Size and Colour: J St.B Gruffedd

PAPERS

White, J.E.J. 1994, *New Trees in a Changing World*. Arboricultural Journal Vol 18 pp 99-112, AB Academic Publishers, London.

White, J.E.J. 1996, *Trees for Community Woodland and Ornamental Plantings in Britain*. In *Landscape Plants* (ed. Thoday, P. & Wilson, J.) Proc. Inst. Hort Conf. Cheltenham 1995 (ISBN 1 86174 002 6).

WEBSITES

Here are some useful websites that will provide additional information.

FUNDING

Royal Forestry Society's website for general information on grant sources at **www.rfs.org.uk/grantsfortrees.asp**

The Big Lottery Fund has an environment funding stream **www.biglottery.org.uk**

The Tree Council has a small grants scheme **www.treecouncil.org.uk**

Groundwork administers various grant schemes **www.groundwork.org.uk**

Entry point for all government grant schemes **www.governmentfunding.org.uk**

Entry point for voluntary sector funding **www.fundinginformation.org.uk**

GOVERNMENT

Biodiversity Action Plans **www.ukbap.org.uk/**

Defra **www.defra.gov.uk**

English Nature **www.english-nature.org.uk**

Highways Agency **www.highways.gov.uk**

Office of the Deputy Prime Minister **www.odpm.gov.uk**

The Forestry Commission **www.forestry.gov.uk**

Scottish Natural Heritage **www.snh.org.uk**

TREE ORGANISATIONS

The Tree Council **www.treecouncil.org.uk**

American Forests **www.americanforests.org**

Ancient Tree Forum **www.woodland-trust.org.uk/ancient-tree-forum**

Arboricultural Association **www.trees.org.uk**

Community Forests **www.communityforest.org.uk**

Institute of Chartered Foresters **www.charteredforesters.org**

International Society of Arboriculture **www.isa-uki.org**

International Tree Foundation **www.internationaltreefoundation.org**

National Forest Company **www.nationalforest.org**

Orchards **www.nat-orchard-forum.org.uk**

Royal Forestry Society **www.rfs.org.uk**

Tree Advice Trust **www.treehelp.info**

Tree Care Industry Association **www.natlarb.com**

Trees for Cities **www.treesforcities.org**

The Woodland Trust **www.woodlandtrust.org.uk**

OTHER ORGANISATIONS

CABE – Commission for Architecture and the Built Environment **www.cabespace.org.uk**

Landscape Institute **www.l-i.org.uk**

VOLUNTARY SECTOR

BTCV (British Trust for Conservation Volunteers) **www.btcv.org.uk**

BEN the Black Environment Network **www.ben-network.org.uk**

Learning Through Landscapes **www.ltl.org.uk**

Royal Horticultural Society **www.rhs.org.uk**

Common Ground **www.commonground.org.uk**

Wildlife Trusts **www.wildlifetrusts.org**